Studies in Speculative Fiction, No. 14

Robert Scholes, Series Editor

Alumni/Alumnae Professor of English and
Chairman, Department of English
Brown University

Other Titles in This Series

The Monster in the Mirror

Gender and the Sentimental/Gothic Myth in *Frankenstein*

The Monster in the Mirror
Gender and the Sentimental/Gothic Myth in *Frankenstein*

by
Mary K. Patterson Thornburg

U·M·I Research Press

Ann Arbor, Michigan

Produced and distributed by
UMI Research Press
an imprint of
University Microfilms, Inc.
Ann Arbor, Michigan 48106

Library of Congress Cataloging in Publication Data

Thornburg, Mary K. Patterson, 1940-
The monster in the mirror.

(Studies in speculative fiction ; no. 14)
Revision of the author's thesis (Ph.D.)—Ball
State University, 1984.
Bibliography: p.
Includes index.
1. Shelley, Mary Wollstonecraft, 1797-1851.
Frankenstein. 2. Monsters in literature. 3. Doubles
in literature. 4. Sex role in literature. 5. Sentiment-
alism in literature. 6. Gothic revival (Literature)
I. Title. II. Series.
PR5397.F73T48 1987   823'.7   87-5560
ISBN 0-8357-1798-4 (alk. paper)

For Gladys Burtch Patterson and Dorothy Hickey Thornburg

Contents

Preface

While many recent writers on *Frankenstein* have used as their text James Rieger's 1974 edition of the novel, which is based upon the 1818 version with appendices indicating Mary Shelley's changes penned into the "Thomas copy" and those later incorporated into the 1831 edition, I have decided to base my reading upon the M. K. Joseph edition, published in 1971, for the following reasons. First, the 1831 revision of *Frankenstein* has been the source of most printings of the novel, and Joseph's is, in my opinion, the best of the recent popular editions to follow that text. Thus the Joseph edition may be, to a general or even an academic audience (since *Frankenstein* is above all a popular novel), more familiar and more readily available than the more scholarly Rieger text. Second, I believe that the later version, representing Mary Shelley's considered decisions about what to change and what to retain in her story, is more likely to satisfy the questions of the author's intent that seem inevitably to be a part of *Frankenstein* scholarship. Thus, while I will occasionally refer to the earlier edition and to Rieger's editorial comments, my references to *Frankenstein* unless otherwise noted will be to the Joseph edition.

I wish to express my gratitude to my professors, Robert Evans, Edward Foster, Tetsumaro Hayashi, Flora Kearney, Frances M. Rippy, Thomas Thornburg, Virginia White, and Richard Whitworth, of the Department of English, Ball State University, and to the School Sisters of Notre Dame, especially Sister M. Alonza.

Introduction

If Victor Frankenstein, laboring compulsively to give shape to the Monster in his "workshop of filthy creation," had not already been at the center of my concern, I think both Victor and the Monster would have occurred to me before long as I struggled to piece together the puzzling relationship between sentimental and Gothic literature. From my first reading of *Frankenstein*, knowing how his ambitious project would turn out, I felt for Victor the same strange mixture of awe, sorrow, and human recognition one feels for Oedipus, eagerly pursuing the knowledge that will fulfill and destroy him. And certainly it was with something akin to pity and terror that I saw my own project taking on unforeseen dimensions: what had begun as a critique of Mary Shelley's book was rapidly becoming an essay on two centuries of popular literature. Unlike Victor, I resisted the urge to flee in horror, but tried instead to give my study some comprehensible size and form. What follows is the result.

As the Monster stands at the center, literally and figuratively, of the novel *Frankenstein* and Victor's tragic quest, all three—the Monster, Victor, and the novel—are to my mind a great figure for something that has been taking shape in our Western culture for over two hundred years, a mythic division that informs not only much of our literature but also our human relationships and our scientific and industrial enterprises. In the following chapters I shall attempt to explore how the sentimental/Gothic myth—a world view divided against itself—evolved, how it took shape, how it is expressed in the novel *Frankenstein*, and how it continues to extend its pervasive influence.

It is the nature of myth to be pervasive: to express the character of a culture in literature, art, and other outward forms, and at the same time to reinforce itself through those forms, ingraining itself in its culture's consciousness, evolving gradually, changing when necessary to accommodate and reflect significant changes in the outward life of the culture, as, for example, the mythos and mythology of northern Europe changed to accommodate the introduction and acceptance of Christianity.

The sentimental/Gothic myth I shall discuss in the next chapters came, both through gradual evolution and less gradual change, to be the dominant world view of Protestant Europe, particularly of England, and of Protestant European settlers and their descendants in America. It is convenient to date the myth's dominance from about the time of the novel's definite emergence, the shift from comedy to sentimental melodrama on the English stage, and the first stirrings of the romantic movement in English poetry—that is, about the middle of the eighteenth century. The sentimental/Gothic myth is distinguishable in a number of ways from the various mythic traditions that preceded it. First, although it is imbued with religiosity and serves, as shall be seen, some of the same purposes as religious myth, it is almost entirely secular—an important characteristic in a religiously heterogeneous culture. Second, it is a myth specifically of the middle classes. Third, it is ostensibly realistic; its literary and dramatic expressions are not only purported to be accurate reflections of contemporary life but are also generally didactic. Finally, and most important, it is a divided myth. Although the sentimental conventions are carried, at least to some degree, into Gothic manifestations of the myth, and although the Gothic, as shall be seen, continually invades and threatens to invade the sentimental manifestations, there is a deep and abiding division between these two mythic sides, a division reflecting a basic dividedness in the cultural character the myth expresses and informs.

So divided, in fact, is the sentimental/Gothic myth that it has been taken for two different and only incidentally related traditions. The first three characteristics just enumerated have seemed to apply only to the sentimental side of the myth, whereas the Gothic has long been taken as an anomaly, a reference (as the term *Gothic* implies) to an earlier time made either for purposes of entertainment and titillation or, by more recent commentators (such as Eino Railo, Mario Praz, Lowry Nelson, Jr., Devendra P. Varma, Leslie Fiedler, and Thomas R. Thornburg), for purposes of archetypal and psychological metaphor. Actually, as I shall attempt to show, the Gothic is the distorted mirror image of the sentimental, reflecting, threatening, and to an extent mocking the conventions of sentimentality.

The division that separates the sentimental side of the myth from the Gothic is a division of consciousness: the sentimental side represents reality as the literate middle class of the Age of Reason wished to see it, and as many actually did (and, as I shall argue, still do) see it. The Gothic embodies those aspects of reality that for many reasons, primarily their irrationality, those same people rejected and continue to reject. That those rejected aspects of reality continued to exist as potent forces is demonstrated by their continued recurrence in Gothic fantasies; there are only two classes of people for whom a ghost story holds no titillation: those who share a culturally sanctioned belief in the existence of ghosts, and those who are convinced, on every conscious and unconscious level, that ghosts do not exist.

The division separating the two sides of the myth from each other is echoed throughout both. The myth's primary metaphor is sexual, or apparently sexual—a code couched in terms of sexual identity and role for perceiving human relationships with and within the objective world. Thus on either side of the divided myth a division between masculinity and femininity governs modes of behavior, modes of perception, even modes of reality as the myth presents reality, so intensely different from each other are masculinity and femininity seen to be.

This masculine/feminine dichotomy has frequently been recognized in studies of eighteenth- and nineteenth-century literature (including some whose main focus is on *Frankenstein*) such as those by Masao Miyoshi, Leslie Fiedler, Kate Ellis, Christopher Small, David Ketterer, and William Veeder. There is little agreement on the exact nature of the dichotomy, however; this is due in part, no doubt, to the complexity of sex-role-reversal material in many of the works studied and, again in part, to the imprecision and overlapping of terminology that must be used (see, for example, Veeder's uses of *feminine, female, effeminate*). But most of the difficulty inherent in a discussion of what I am calling a "masculine/feminine dichotomy" lies, I am convinced, in the very currency of the myth in our own time. While it will be my contention that the sentimental/Gothic myth has in large part defined what we mean when we say masculine or feminine, I am bound, in my discussion of that definition process, to use those terms as they are currently understood. The lack of agreement among writers who recognize the masculine/feminine dichotomy, and the frequently confusing use of terms, stem for the most part from the difficulty of getting far enough outside the myth to view it at all objectively.

In the chapters that follow, I shall attempt to deal with the particular problem of gender-related language by defining certain terms as my argument encounters them, and by using them thereafter only in the senses that I have defined for them. This, I realize, will not guarantee my objectivity (or the reader's), but will perhaps help to make a distinction that must be made between actual human beings, both male and female, and the men and women of sentimenal/Gothic myth, who are basically metaphorical figures, bearing only a minimal resemblance to real people as they existed in the eighteenth or nineteenth century or as they exist in the twentieth.

Another problem of terminology should be addressed. Throughout my discussion of the sentimental/Gothic myth I shall be using the term "conscious" to describe the sentimental side of the divided myth and "unconscious" in connection with the Gothic side. By this usage I do not mean to suggest that those who expressed the myth in literature or art, or who contributed to its structure, were conscious of the mythic nature of the conventions they dealt with, except inasmuch as certain authors of antisentimental works (such as Jane Austen) realized the conventions were conventions. Myth, by its nature, is *not* self-conscious, although one might argue that an artist working with mythic material can often sense its potency. By my use of these terms, I mean merely to suggest that the conventions of the sentimental tradition were consciously accepted by most members of the culture, while the Gothic conventions, representing aspects of reality consciously and unconsciously suppressed by the culture, were almost entirely unrecognized as being in any way related either to accepted conventions or to the "real lives" of human beings.

In the literature of the sentimental/Gothic myth, as we shall see, one seldom finds either side of the myth manifested purely. There are good reasons why this is true. First among them is the nature of the Gothic as a completion of the sentimental, a body of material unacceptable to the conscious sentimental tradition but complementary to it. While Gothic elements are rejected by the sentimental tradition, whose purpose is to reflect and reinforce the rationality, morality, and controlled emotionality of its culture, the reverse is in no way true; the Gothic does not reject the sentimental. The Gothic side of the myth represents an unconscious acknowledgment of the potency of these rejected elements, an unconscious need within the culture to deal with reality in its entirety, not merely with those parts of it that are consciously safe and acceptable. Thus the Gothic is in a very literal sense *monstrous;* it is a warning to the sentimental, a demonstration of its own existence. As such, it tends to appear, if only briefly, sometimes almost perversely, even within the most determinedly sentimental expressions—as, for example, certain scenes of real Gothic intensity occur within Lewis Carroll's Alice books, where the author's conscious control of his sentimental material apparently weakens enough (perhaps at the prompting of his artistic instincts) to allow the substratum of Gothic horror to surface momentarily.

On the other hand, within those works that are frank expressions of the Gothic there is no need to reject the sentimental; in fact, from the artistic as well as from what might be called the Gothic point of view, there is every reason to allow the sentimental free entry, to seek it out. Since the Gothic functions as a warning to the sentimental, it is most effective when it exists in the same vicinity, on the same plane. Gothic figures can exist and act within their own Gothic milieu, as Ambrosio and Matilda do in certain scenes of *The Monk,* but they are more commonly found, and more effective, in the company of sentimental figures they can threaten. No doubt this is true partly for artistic reasons; the point-of-view character or characters are usually sentimental, perhaps simply because the sentimental point of view is the more familiar and—to the reader—the more trustworthy of the two. But there is another reason why the sentimental is almost always—if not always—

included in expressions of the Gothic. Without its sentimental counterpart and target, the Gothic is not only ineffective but unsupported, lacking in purpose; it has no reason to exist. Just as Frankenstein's Monster is superfluous without his creator, the Gothic half of the sentimental/Gothic myth is superfluous in the absence of the sentimental.

While it is indeed unlikely, for the reasons just mentioned, that many purely Gothic manifestations of the myth have been produced, it is reasonable to expect, for the same reasons, that works of pure sentimentality might have appeared (and might continue to appear in twentieth-century guise) with some frequency. Given the didacticism characteristic of the sentimental side of the myth, and given the determination of sentimentality to represent itself as complete, to reject and deny the reality of the Gothic, one might assume that numerous expressions of pure sentimentality would be available for examination. As a matter of fact, such expressions are available (though by no means all or even a large percentage of those published remain in print), but they are of little value in criticism because of their unfamiliarity to the general reader or literary scholar. Most of those purely sentimental works of earlier centuries that have remained in any sense alive for the reading public are thought of, or were frankly intended, as children's books, and even these are preserved, one suspects, only as curiosities or out of affection. One such work that expresses almost all the conventions of sentimentality without any Gothic or antisentimental ingredients to temper them is *Mother Carey's Chickens* by Kate Douglas Wiggin, the predictable story of a brave mother guiding her brood of insufferably precious children through various tribulations and disasters. The book is interesting primarily for its display of the sentimental myth unadulterated, but also for the somewhat amazing consideration that it was once a "classic," among the best of its genre. In the later twentieth century, certain "family" films and television series have been pure, or nearly pure, expressions of the sentimental myth, but the best of these are memorable not for their sentimentality but for their playing *against* the sentimental conventions.

Most sentimental works with enough artistic merit to survive are well diluted, often with Gothic elements. But throughout the period of the sentimental/Gothic myth's dominance, an antisentimental strain has also appeared, especially in serious literary works but also in more ephemeral productions such as some of the film and television examples mentioned above. Even at the beginning of the sentimental/Gothic period, of course, certain works remained outside the tradition of the myth or used the terms of the myth in a parodic or debunking fashion; Henry Fielding's novels, for example, both skirt the sentimental tradition *(Tom Jones)* and parody it *(Shamela),* while *Joseph Andrews* begins as a parody but soon moves, for the most part, outside the territory of the myth. Other works, however, while they remain within the tradition of sentimental/Gothic myth, derive much of their strength from the inclusion of antisentimental elements and devices. Such works play off their readers' expectations of sentimental characters and situations in order to introduce other characters, situations, and outcomes that are distinctly unorthodox in terms of the sentimental tradition. Jane Austen and William Thackeray are two outstanding examples of writers who produced works in the antisentimental tradition. And even such a profoundly sentimental writer as Louisa May Alcott included strong antisentimental elements in her best work, accounting perhaps for much of its continued popular appeal.

Thus, in examining each side of the sentimental/Gothic myth, one must recognize the dilution that occurs within works exemplifying both sides: sentimental elements appear within the Gothic, Gothic elements within the sentimental, and a strong antisentimental strain emerges at times within both. The works I shall use to illustrate both the sentimental and Gothic traditions will, I hope, be familiar enough to the reader that the abstractions they exemplify will be illustrated concretely and that these, in turn, will suggest further examples from the reader's literary experience.

Even before I have defined the terms and discussed examples of the sentimental/Gothic myth, the reader will no doubt have begun to anticipate my argument for *Frankenstein* as a remarkably apt example of and figure for the myth. As a novel (and I shall argue that the book is properly termed a novel, not a romance, despite its effectiveness as an extended metaphor), *Frankenstein* contains both sentimental and antisentimental elements, but its main thrust is Gothic, as the Gothic Monster emerges early in the book to reflect, mock, and threaten the sentimental ambitions not only of Victor Frankenstein but of the other characters as well. The central situation of the book—Victor's creation of the Monster and the subsequent conflict between them—is a division that echoes the sentimental/Gothic split. Victor Frankenstein, "self-devoted" and self-concious sentimental hero, creates and rejects the Monster; I shall argue that creation and rejection are here essentially the same act, for it is Victor's intention to perfect *himself* as the ideal man of sentimental tradition, and in doing so he casts out of himself those elements the sentimental tradition abhors, the very elements that make up the Monster. The Monster's independent existence, like the persistent vitality of the Gothic tradition, affirms the potency of those elements. And the Monster's subsequent peculiar relationship with Victor, a mixture of violence, threat, and devotion, is—like the relationship of the Gothic to the sentimental—an ambiguous affirmation of the fact that neither side is complete without the other, while their separation portends the destruction of one and the other's loss of meaning, loss of reason to exist.

Moreover, in the act of creation and rejection, both Victor and his creature are further divided, like the sentimental/Gothic myth, along masculine/feminine lines as Victor, the conscious embodiment of the sentimental ideal, draws those lines. Victor's creation of the Monster is the culmination of his adolescence, the act that marks his coming of age in a family that is a model of the sentimental ideal (at least in Victor's eyes—but also, ironically, in Mary Shelley's, for Victor's family is revealed to the reader as possessing all the flaws of the sentimental side of the myth, while falling far short of the perfection Victor claims for it). Thus the masculine/feminine dichotomy apparent in the characters of Victor and the Monster is dictated by the sentimental/Gothic myth, for the myth's terms are Victor's moral standard, his only notion of religion or honor, his guide to attaining manhood.

Victor chooses the dichotomy consciously to the extent that he chooses to create the Monster; and he recognizes it consciously to the extent that, upon encountering the Monster as a living being, he reacts as one would to a nightmare: he rejects his creation, flees from it, and attempts to forget about it. Victor knows at once that the Monster is his own bad dream (its awakening is connected by him to a literal nightmare), and he knows that the content of the dream is personal, domestic, and sexual (the nightmare has him embracing his fiancée who turns in his arms into the corpse of his mother). Being who he is, however, Victor is never *fully* aware of the Monster's meaning or of the Monster's relationship to his own identity. That awareness is left, as we shall see, to the Monster.

That the creation of the Monster is in reality a division, that the Monster and Victor are doubles, and that other sets of doubles occur throughout *Frankenstein* as throughout Gothic literature generally, are widely recognized. The doppelgänger is so common a figure in Gothic fiction, poetry, and art, in fact, that it is often classed with other Gothic standbys, like the ruined castle or the moldering crypt, as a standard piece of paraphernalia— loaded with symbolic significance for some critics, to others nothing but a well-worn piece of stage equipment. A few writers, like Masao Miyoshi, recognize division and the double as figures for a widespread cultural phenomenon; Miyoshi says that self-division was "endemic" in the nineteenth century (ix–x).

Others interpret the Victor/Monster doubling (and in some cases the other instances of doubling they see in *Frankenstein*) in various ways. Muriel Spark, a biographer of Mary Shelley, says the Monster represents "reason in isolation," having been produced by Victor's "obsessional rational effort" (137); Spark credits Richard Church, an earlier biographer, with having suggested the idea to her. To Harold Bloom, "Frankenstein is the mind and emotions turned in upon themselves, and his creature is the mind and emotions turned imaginatively outward..." (122). Psychological readings of *Frankenstein*, such as that by Morton Kaplan and Robert Kloss, explain the Monster as the agent of Victor's unconscious, committing those acts that the conscious Victor cannot or will not commit; Kate Ellis calls the Monster "the part of himself [Victor] cannot or will not bring home" (137).

A number of writers (for example, Small, U. C. Knoepflmacher, Ellen Moers, Veeder) are led by the correspondences between *Frankenstein* and Mary Shelley's life, especially her relationship with Shelley, to identify the doubles with Mary, Shelley, and various members of their family and circle of acquaintances. Shelley had used Victor as a pen name, and as a name for characters evidently based upon himself; William, the name of Victor Frankenstein's murdered brother, is also the name of Mary's father, her half-brother, and her son, and was even used for Mary herself in correspondence between her parents before her birth; other possible identifications of fictional characters with actual people abound. Furthermore, the idea of two people united as one entity (or of one person divided into two) is so frequently encountered in Shelley's writing that these correspondences between Mary's and Shelley's lives and *Frankenstein* are almost inevitably linked to the idea of the double. Such biographical identifications obviously involve complexities in the assignment of sexual roles. Commonly, critics see either Victor or the Monster as representing the female, or feminine, or effeminate half of the double, while the other is thought to represent the male, or masculine half.

That there is evidence to support *both* of these views suggests to me that neither is entirely correct, although each view may be partly right. For example, one need not reject Ellen Moers's reading of the creation of the Monster as a "birth myth," in which Victor is a figure for the mother, to admit the validity of Knoepflmacher's suggestion that the Monster embodies Mary's hostility toward William Godwin (Victor) or of Veeder's that Victor reacts to the Monster's appearance at his bedside as a maiden would to an attempted seduction. And yet, it is easier to see the validity of all of these varied readings if one can see the Victor/Monster relationship as something complex and far-reaching enough to encompass them all.

In my discussion, I shall argue that Victor's creation of the Monster and the subsequent relationship between the two represent not a strict male/female division, nor even a strict masculine/feminine (or masculine/effeminate) division—nor an identification of either character with any particular person, though biographical correspondences are certainly to be found—but rather a rejection of a set of qualities seen as unacceptable in a man by the sentimental tradition and thus by Victor himself. These qualities include "excessively masculine" traits, as we shall see— violence, willfulness, sexual passion, gross physicality—but they also include "unmanly" (that is, feminine) traits. Thus, as I shall attempt to demonstrate,

Victor himself becomes depleted—masculine, but in a sense emasculated and drained of his unacknowledged feminine qualities as well—while the Monster, divided from Victor, is just as incomplete but is an opposing, distorted reflection of Victor.

As recently as 1986, the author of a serious study of *Frankenstein* felt compelled to ask that his readers "put aside preconceptions about [Mary Shelley's] ineptitude" long enough to consider whether his claims for specific points of critical interpretation might fit into a view of the novel as a coherent work (Veeder, 4–5). For a book that seems to so thorough and recent a critic to require such a plea for fairness (and most of the best recent criticism is careful to acknowledge supposed flaws in the work), *Frankenstein* has attracted what would seem to be a surprising amount of serious critical attention.

Two general observations about this recent criticism might be noted. One is that there is a wide diversity of opinion about the significance of the novel and about what the "Frankenstein metaphor," as George Levine calls the creation of the Monster, means. Much of this diversity may be explained as resulting from differences in critical method, no doubt. But more than methodological differences are involved when the same book can be argued as *primarily* a "Mystery play" whose "deep-structured subject" is "the Trinitarian Question" (Wilt, 33); a "birth myth...lodged in the novelist's imagination... by the fact that she was herself a mother" (Moers, 79); a love-hate fantasy whose central relationship is that between Mary (the Monster) and her father (Victor Frankenstein) (Knoepflmacher); an "analysis of domestic affection" in the context of "the bourgeois family" (Ellis, 124); an anti-Godwinian, antirevolutionary political critique (Sterrenburg); a literary dream telling (Stevick); the first science fiction novel (Scholes and Rabkin, Aldiss, and others); "one of the most vivid versions we have of the Romantic mythology of the self" (Bloom, 122); and so on. This list is by no means exhaustive. While I do not claim that these categorizations are necessarily mutually exclusive, I would suggest that the variety of interpretations *Frankenstein* seems not only to invite but to support is itself a facet of the novel worthy of analysis.

A second notable characteristic of *Frankenstein* criticism is the tendency of writers to deplore various flaws in the book without agreeing upon the identity or the nature of the flaws. The first reviews of the novel, after its publication in 1818, were in a way prophetic of the tone later criticism would take. Even those readers who were enthusiastic in *Frankenstein*'s favor expressed serious misgivings amounting almost to apologies for their enthusiasm, while those most violently opposed to it nevertheless admitted that it aroused in them a certain reluctant admiration or fascination. The tone of recent criticism is just as intense, but as writers interpret the central meaning of the novel in very different ways, they also find very different faults in it. In general, nineteenth-century criticism expressed shock and disgust at the story itself but praised the author's craft; recent critics have more or less reversed this position, admiring the content but not the form, and, as Veeder notes, charging to Mary Shelley's "ineptitude" as a writer those facets of the book their criticism does not explain. While one writer, for example, will find the Robert Walton frame contrived and superfluous, others see it as thematically important. While plot coincidences (the Monster's meeting with young William, Victor's encountering Walton) and apparent discrepancies (Victor's failure to mention Justine until he describes Elizabeth's letter in which she is mentioned) seem to some to be evidence of Mary Shelley's inexperience, others cite them as evidence of her artistry. On the whole, as Veeder's plea for fairness suggests, *Frankenstein* has attracted a kind of obligatory fault finding; critics seem unwilling to give this book a completely fair hearing, even though they insist upon its importance.

I believe there is a significant reason for this critical attitude. *Frankenstein*, I think, touches a nerve in most readers that is extremely sensitive; it threatens the reader's objectivity. Thus even the most admiring reader is uncomfortable with the book until he or she has demonstrated superiority by finding some obvious flaw in it. For example, the brief appearance and immediate disappearance of Victor's brother Ernest—who is mentioned in Elizabeth's first letter to Victor and never thereafter—is a puzzling, though not a glaring, apparent discrepancy in the plot. Veeder sees Ernest's "escape" from the Monster's revenge as a psychological escape route that Mary, identifying with the name Ernest, left for herself in her implied criticism of Shelley and their relationship. Without denying this possibility, it seems to me that, on another level, Ernest's survival is a subtle hint that the Frankenstein name survives, just as the Monster's possible survival is implied at the end of the book. Yet most critics who mention Ernest at all, as Veeder says, see this problem not as an aspect of the novel that deserves critical examination but as a sign of Mary's artistic immaturity—even though she carefully revised other equally minor details between the 1818 and 1831 editions. This, I think, is those readers' own "escape route." The book's early reviewers were in a way fortunate; they could admit, as most twentieth-century critics and scholars cannot, to negative emotional reactions. Whether or not their shock was produced, as they apparently believed, by the sacrilege of Victor's "presumption" in creating a living being is beside the point; the point is that they were not obliged to pretend a sophisticated moral and emotional acceptance in the face of something that aroused emotional antipathy. They were able to reject the book on the basis of contemporary moral standards and so had no need, as modern readers have, to shift their objections to formal grounds.

It seems to me that both of the more recent reactions—the varied and exclusive interpretations, the obligatory objection to some aspect of the book's form—are similarly motivated. To concentrate the burden of proof for interpretation on a narrow and often peripheral aspect of the novel is to avoid a confrontation with an emotionally repellent whole; to find the author's execution of the work clumsy or incompetent is to express a personal rejection of the novel without taking an unfashionable or inadmissable critical stance.

What is there in *Frankenstein* that prompts such a reaction? Compared with other Gothic novels, it is not particularly macabre, nor can the idea of Frankenstein's presumption be considered especially shocking, at least to twentieth-century readers; why does it remain so fascinating and so disturbing? I am convinced—and in the following chapters I shall attempt to demonstrate—that the source of *Frankenstein*'s power is its delineation and merciless exposure of the sentimental/Gothic myth, our culture's dominant world view at least until the middle of the twentieth century. The myth's dualities are both terrible and terribly familiar: the duality of power and powerlessness; the duality of will (presumption) and the loss of will (compulsion); the dualities of good and bad intent, of self-knowledge and self-ignorance, of creativity and destructiveness; and above all the duality of sexual identity and role. *Frankenstein*, although in many ways a representative work of the early nineteenth century, is not yet a period piece to be contemplated from a comfortable position outside its frame. Whether we like to think so or not, as twentieth-century readers we are in a very real sense still within that frame.

1

The Sentimental/Gothic Myth

Mythic Self-Division: Origins and Implications

Frankenstein—indeed, the Gothic novel in general and the Gothic element in other literary works—is an expression of the dark side, the largely unconscious but terribly potent underlying reality, of a sentimental/Gothic myth that had become a controlling world view in England, the Protestant countries of western Europe, and America during the late eighteenth and entire nineteenth centuries. The myth, although it encompasses far more than sexual relationships, is shaped by a perception of sexual identity and role. Because this particular world view has been so overwhelmingly influential on the life and art of the West for almost two-and-a-half centuries, our very familiarity with its terms may lead us to assume that we understand the myth's structure; in fact, however, it still holds enough potency for us that we may have some difficulty in discovering its real shape and discerning its far-reaching significance. For this reason, I wish to examine in some detail the roots, the nature, and the implications of this world view.

The sentimental/Gothic myth, reflecting and reinforcing the cultural climate of its time and supplanting earlier world views whose religious centrality and sociopolitical assumptions had become outdated, developed on two sides or levels so apparently incongruous that they have frequently been seen as only incidentally related to each other. On the conscious level—whence sprang the conventions reflected in sentimental literature and the code of manners and morality implied therein—the myth pretended to a high-minded idealization of feeling and a pious, if often self-serving, regard for the virtues of domesticity. It exalted moral and societal virtues associated primarily with the Protestant middle class; it became, in fact, a sort of pseudoreligion, a set of secular beliefs and imperatives that spanned the religious lines drawn in the sixteenth and seventeenth centuries and supplanted to a large extent the religious authority exercised by the church before the Protestant Reformation.

The myth was in expression often consciously didactic, establishing proprieties and scales of value in certain areas of conduct—mainly domestic and other close personal relationships, but to an extent in all interpersonal dealings—as well as in the subjective experiences that inform conduct: emotions, natural inclinations, intellectual perceptions. Because the myth, inasmuch as it was consciously perceived, concerned itself primarily with human relationships within and immediately tangential to the domestic area, the terms of its expression were characteristically sexual, or perceived as sexual, in content. The conscious, sentimental side of the myth (to which I shall refer as the *sentimental tradition*) stressed a conscious "separation of male and female spheres of activity" (Ellis, 124), a separation of masculine and feminine *genders* (for the sexual terms were actually metaphorical, referring in fact to behavior that had little to do with literal sexuality or sexual differences). The separation was so pervasive and so complete that the two sexes were viewed mythically almost as two different species of being; and this separation came to be seen as the basis of a natural order on which human civilization rested, an order necessary to the moral, psychological, and physical well-being of real individuals.

Underlying the conscious level of the myth, however, was another, darker level where masculinity and femininity became more obviously metaphoric conditions, expressing a fatal polarity, a drama of violent conquest and submission taking place in all areas of human experience: not only domestic and social, but also political, cultural, economic, intellectual, and scientific. Both sides of the myth, although one was largely unconscious (but all the stronger for that reason), were of immeasurable influence on the personal and historic events of European and American culture for the period of the myth's endurance and evolution—a period that, as shall be seen, still persists.

What I am here calling a myth may be defined as a widely accepted weltanschauung, a way or set of ways for perceiving the nature of self and reality. The sentimental/Gothic myth dominated Western culture from about the middle of the eighteenth century until at least the beginning of the twentieth, and its influence is still far from weak; when one reflects, for example, upon how deeply assumptions based on the myth pervaded the work of Sigmund Freud, the strength of its hold on our time becomes apparent. As with any such dominant, culture-shaping world view, the nature of this one can be known only from the evidence of its reflections in the manners, choices, and actions in which it is implicitly stated, in the "documents" it produces, especially in literature. In England, the onset of the sentimental/Gothic myth can be seen in a number of remarkable changes that took place almost simultaneously in literature: the birth of the novel and its swift ascendancy as the most popular of literary forms; the decline of dramatic literature from Restoration and early eighteenth-century heights into a long period of essentially mediocre melodrama; and of course the whole poetic revolution that we call romanticism. Another change, long ignored or deprecated, was the rise of the Gothic mode, both in works that it dominated and as a secondary but insistent element in other literature.

The complex reasons for these particular changes in literary form, content, style, and reception are interwoven with those historical and cultural changes that marked the ascendancy of the sentimental/Gothic myth. In two further sections of this chapter I shall examine the characteristic conventions of the sentimental and Gothic sides of the myth, conventions that reflect the separateness but also the interdependency of the two sides or traditions. First, however, let us look at the historical and cultural conditions under which the myth arose, the ways in which it evolved from the world view that preceded it, and the reasons for the development of its particular characteristics.

The origins of the sentimental/Gothic myth are in great part responsible for its characteristic divisions and apparent contradictions. Although the myth emerged in the eighteenth century, it is related to a world view—the myth of courtly love—that had preceded it, reaching its heights in the late Middle Ages to decline during the Renaissance and virtually disappear in the sixteenth and seventeenth centuries when its relevance was lost. A basically secular myth—although outwardly professing adherence to Protestant beliefs—the sentimental/Gothic myth nonetheless bears traces of earlier religious influences. And, ostensibly a faithful reflection of the realities of human nature and experience, still the myth necessarily served as a metaphorical vehicle for psychological and archetypal aspects of reality that its adherents were reluctant or unable to deal with consciously.

The myth arose as Western culture was attempting to absorb world-shaking changes in religion, politics, economics, scientific knowledge, and philosophy that had been engendered in the Renaissance to reverberate through at least three centuries, a "transitional" period whose very length attests to the magnitude of the changes and the resistance offered in the face of them. During these years, assumptions that had seemed unchangeable were first questioned and then overthrown, and the "realities" upon which these assumptions had been based, even the reality of geography itself, were swept away. Yet certain aspects of tradition could not be rooted out: attitudes and beliefs that seemed unreasonable to the new, "enlightened" order were driven into different forms to move darkly and unacknowledged among the new symbols of European culture. Certain aspects of the older traditions needed, in fact, to be preserved if the process of enlightenment were not to overcome the continuity of the civilization upon which it was acting.

One of the most basic and wide-reaching changes to occur between the fifteenth and eighteenth centuries was the change from conservative feudalism to the revolutionary, individualistic system of capitalism. Under the former system wealth and influence were concentrated in the feudal lord (and the reigning monarch was, in effect, the most powerful of these lords), so that every individual depended for his economic and social position and betterment upon the feudal hierarchy. This situation was reflected in the courtly love myth, where the important relationship is between the knight and the lord, symbolically represented (for reasons that will be examined presently) as a relationship between the knight and the lady, the lord's consort.

When feudal power diminished and land inheritance became a means by which members of the middle classes could accumulate wealth and gain individual power, the individual's own family took on a different status. Women had always represented marriagable property, but political, economic, and religious factors now combined to make the consideration even more important than it had been in earlier centuries, and at the same time to make a different set of qualities important or desirable in women themselves. In 1660 and 1688, as Christopher Hill documents in his essay "Clarissa Harlowe and Her Times," political compromises reflecting a reaction against the power of the landed classes in England reduced landowners' opportunities for competition in the increasingly capitalistic economy, and had far-reaching effects on middle-class society and the family.

Marriage became especially important as a means of consolidating the larger land holdings necessary to retain or increase wealth, since the system of inheritance had replaced traces of feudalism that political upheaval had effectively destroyed. Strict authority of parents over daughters, or of the eldest son over his sisters, was needed in order to assure marriages contracted to the economic advantage of the family; such authority "had its economic basis in the father's ability to grant or withhold marriage portions to his daughters" (Hill, 114–15). At the same time, the economic rise of the bourgeoisie resulted in the creation of a leisured class of women, who were expected to acquire accomplishments and graces formerly restricted to the aristocracy. Such acquisitions increased a woman's status on what was, quite frankly, the marriage market; undoubtedly, however, they made her less likely than ever to accept so frankly economic a view of herself and her attainments.

Even more valuable in a woman than evidence of her cultural accomplishments was her chastity. As Hill explains,

> In the Puritan conception fidelity in the wife, and premarital chastity, began to be insisted on with a new vehemence. Since love was ideally the basis of marriage, then the marriage must be inviolate. In practice in most marriages property was still the main consideration; and in the world of capitalist production expensive goods must not be shop-soiled or tarnished. (115)

With the increased importance of the inheritance system, chastity was absolutely necessary to ensure an unbroken male line. Thus, with the new system of economic values, the adulterous love celebrated in the courtly love myth between knight and lady, or even the relative sexual freedom condoned in the sixteenth and seventeenth centuries, was unthinkable. However, Hill's explanation illustrates the basis for a duplicity to be found in the sentimental tradition: in a Protestant culture the virtue of chastity must be regarded in a religious or moral light, with the same morality to be observed by men and women alike; but in a capitalist, landowning system the chastity of women is important quite apart from moral considerations, while the sexual behavior of men is to a great degree regulated by economic conditions that make marriage an essentially practical, economically motivated relationship.

As economic considerations made middle-class women particularly dependent upon and subordinate to men, even as the same considerations encouraged an *apparent* improvement in women's educational and social status, so the mythic view of women that had been upheld during the period of the courtly love myth had largely lost its power by the end of the seventeenth century. Such comfort and protection as medieval Catholicism had afforded women was long gone, and while the Protestant Reformation had promised them a status, in the eyes of the church, more nearly equal to that of men, in practice this promise was little honored. As Hill notes, "the protestant sects attributed divine inspiration to the letter of the Bible, newly translated into the vernacular for all to read; and the Bible is explicit on the subordination of women" (118). Practically, too, the alternative that Catholicism had provided for poor women, and for unmarried women of all classes—the convent—was now unavailable. The real consequence of the Reformation for women was thus not a happy one: "The Virgin," says Hill, "was no longer at the right hand of her Son to intercede for her sex. In her place stood St. Paul and the Patriarchs" (118). And in the place of the religious community stood nothing at all. A woman's marriageability depended largely upon her economic, not her personal, attractiveness; and for those women not fortunate enough to find husbands there awaited, at worst, brutal sexual and economic exploitation, and at best a dreary and ridiculous dependency.

Other changes, less immediate than those in political, economic, and religious structures but just as far-reaching, were felt as well during the centuries between the fifteenth and eighteenth. Knowledge about the nature of the world had increased immensely, through technological advances that widened the geographical boundaries of the known world and allowed new discoveries about the nature of that world. These discoveries, shaking the foundations of what had been believed about reality for centuries, both encouraged the secularization of knowledge and deprived people of the comfortable assurances hitherto provided by the apparent agreement between religious faith and scientific knowledge. They rendered the old world view, upon which the arts and literature of the West were based, impotent and obsolete; at the same time they made some sort of new and unifying world view imperative.

The courtly love myth, itself bearing traces of a pre-Christian mythos along with a symbolism long associated with medieval Christianity, had been built upon a sexual metaphor; and it was from the reshaping of this metaphor that the sentimental/Gothic myth, troubled and revolutionary, emerged. The vocabulary of Western myth changed with the toppling of the immense power of religious and economic feudalism and the revolution in scientific knowledge; and the loss of the old mythic structure, too, was a most potent factor in the shaping of the new one.

Given a substantial dogmatic faith, says C. G. Jung, the archetypes of that faith "absorb" the entire collective unconscious (60). The Jungian concept of a strongly accepted organized body of mythology as a depository for the symbolic life of the individual psyche, and of the individual's struggle to deal with unconscious forces once organized dogma no longer serves to contain them, is especially relevant in regard to the monumental cultural shift under discussion here. The life of the unconscious, says Jung, seeks established dogma and ritual for its symbols, which form a bulwark against the "uncanny, living depths of the world and of the psyche" (60). Ritual and myth, until the Reformation, had allowed individuals to project powerful psychic elements, including the female principle described by Jung as *anima,* the male principle *animus,* and the demonic principle he calls the *shadow,* onto symbols far enough removed from the individual—and well enough established in dogmatic tradition—to leave the individual psyche in relative safety from their incursion upon it. The courtly love tradition, closely bound up as it was with Christian and pre-Christian symbols, elevated its figures of good and evil, its symbols for the anima and animus, into an allegorical and magical realm explicitly above and apart from actual human experience.

The disappearance of that tradition, however, forced the archetypes back, as it were, into the "real" world of the individual. This being, in Jungian terms, an intolerable situation, a new dogma—the mythic structure underlying sentimental/Gothic literature—was formed. But the new structure was not seen as dogma or ritual; rather it was supposed to replace the formal dogma and ritual the Reformation had rejected and to conform to a rational view of the world. Thus the archetypes became deeply divided, projecting themselves onto society and the individual as sexual and social roles that were supposed to represent rational and conscious reality, but also submerging themselves within individuals' unconscious to reappear, eventually, as the new symbols of the Gothic tradition.

While the courtly love myth allowed individuals to distinguish between the ritual acceptance of that myth and the ordinary circumstances of their lives, the new mythic structure took its shape from pressure created by the forcing of archetypal symbols onto ordinary human beings and their relationships. Jung stresses the impossibility of dealing satisfactorily with the unconscious on a conscious level, without an accepted body of myth to accommodate its seemingly superhuman, "uncanny" forces. The creation of a world view to replace the deposed one was inevitable; but, since the new myth purported to be a model of the actual world, above all rational, its unacknowledged contradictions and its division into a light and dark side were inevitable as well.

Other writers have connected the courtly love myth with the sentimental and Gothic traditions. Leslie Fiedler, in *Love and Death in the American Novel,* correctly insists that the place of woman—or, more accurately, of the female principle—is finally the basic issue of each myth. But Fiedler, in terming the change from the courtly love to the new mythic structure a reversal from dread of the female principle to an exaltation of it, seems to me to misread the new myth by assuming a complete separation of the sentimental from the Gothic; he overlooks their essential relationship as two parts of the same whole. Fiedler sees the Lady of the courtly love myth as a basically dark figure because of the element of incest with which she is almost invariably associated; he claims that the sentimental tradition reverses this position in that it elevates women to a clearly superior status. In fact, the female figure in both mythic traditions is far more ambiguous than Fiedler's analysis suggests. The dread of the female principle that he finds in the older tradition was intermixed with both reverence and hostility; in the new myth the reverence so apparent in sentimental expressions is drastically undermined by the hostility of the Gothic, and because of the new myth's ostensible reflection of factual reality the effect on the lives of contemporary women was disastrous.

Fiedler holds that the courtly love myth was a "true counterreligion to Christianity," which, however, "the Catholic Church was able to deal with ... in its immemorial way, absorbing it into the cult of the Virgin" (19). The very existence of a Virgin "cult" in medieval Christianity would seem to be evidence that the mythic female principle, in its light aspect at least but probably also colored by the dread associated with the courtly love Lady, was already a part of established Christian tradition—as indeed we know it was, having been introduced into Europe through Byzantine Christianity. The dark aspect of the female principle is implicitly acknowledged in the very hostility toward women expressed by orthodox Pauline Christianity, drawing support from the Biblical figure of Eve in Christian tradition, but also based, no doubt, on the struggles between followers of ancient goddess cults and the patriarchal peoples who eventually supplanted them. Thus, while the idealization of woman in courtly love tradition may have represented a resurgence of the female principle, this attitude cannot be seen as essentially opposed to Christian tradition. Nor can the idealized woman of the courtly love myth, especially as she was identified with the Virgin, be said to represent mainly the dark aspect of the female principle.

In fact, the Lady idealized in the poems of courtly love is always an ambiguous figure. Never completely separate from the idea of the Virgin, and thus never wholly the dark woman, she is nonetheless in many ways forbidding, unapproachable. For the traditional reverence given the Virgin is expressed in terms of filial devotion, whereas the Lady of courtly love is addressed as the beloved. This aspect of the myth is, of course, inseparable from the ancient goddess worship reflected in the Christian elevation of Mary, but in reasserting it the makers of the courtly love myth necessarily reintroduced the element of incest, which was and is the chief source of the ambiguous light in which the ancient goddesses, and the Lady of courtly love, must be seen.

If the courted Lady is in any sense a figure for the Virgin—the accepted mother-figure of the Christian world—then the lover who courts her is also her son, and small wonder that his courtship is conducted with apparent reluctance to achieve its consummation. Nor is it surprising that the Lady herself should come to share in the darkness that such a courtship involves. The fact that the unconsciously incestuous worship of the goddess-figure was here invoked in a consciously patriarchal, feudal culture would tend not only to increase the guilt associated with such a contemplated relationship, but would also tend to change the way in which the Lady was regarded as dark. In a patriarchal system, the offended authority is not the Lady herself, but rather her consort, the feudal Lord who stands in a position of fatherly authority over the lover. The Lady must be as much a sinner against such authority as the courtly lover himself—more so, in fact, from the point of view of the lover, who must project guilt away from himself to avoid anxiety at the prospect of invoking the wrath, and losing the protection, of the strong father-figure.

The incestuous nature of the courtly love relationship is enough in itself to cast a shadow of ambiguity over the relationship and over the Lady herself; however, the shadow deepens when it is seen that the dark and light ladies are the same and are inseparable. In the ancient myth of the goddess cults, in the courtly love myth, and in the sentimental/Gothic myth that follows it, the female figure who stands for the female principle is seen as an incestuous love object, thereby inspiring contradictory emotions, attraction and repulsion, at once. There is indeed a difference between the nature of the incestuous relationship as it is found in the myth of courtly love and as it is seen in the sentimental/Gothic myth, as I shall suggest in my discussion of the incest theme within the newer myth, but the difference is not a reversal from dread to exaltation of the female figure. It is true that the woman of the sentimental/Gothic myth seems on the surface to be all light, but one must recognize that the dark side, the woman seen in a negative way, has merely been disguised. The reason for this disguise, the apparent (but only apparent) discarding of the "dark" female principle, is to be found in the nature of the new myth, which unlike the courtly love myth does not provide a safe and comforting distance between the individual psyche and the mythic symbols.

It must be remembered that in both the courtly love myth and the sentimental/Gothic myth, the theme of love—of courtship and sexuality—is essentially metaphoric. Denis de Rougemont, in *Love in the Western World,* argues that the love expressed in "the great European myth of adultery"—the *Tristan and Iseult* romance—was not that of the lovers for each other but was in fact a love of the state of being in love, a love of passion, of suffering, and finally a love and courtship of death. Rougemont, it seems, argues of the courtly love myth approximately what I am claiming of the later myth, that it is more than (and other than) it appears on the surface and is popularly thought to be, that it conceals its own "Gothic" darknesses. Rougemont, in fact, asserts that any myth arises necessarily, in part, because of a need to conceal a truth that cannot be directly acknowledged: *"A myth is needed to express the dark and unmentionable fact that passion is linked with death"* (10). In Rougemont's analysis, this "dark and unmentionable fact" is both expressed and disguised by literary devices such as symbolism, e.g., Tristan's bared sword lying between the adulterous lovers. It is my contention that, although such concealing devices operate to some extent in both the sentimental and Gothic sides of the later myth, these devices alone were not strong enough to keep the dark truths disguised, to keep them from invading the conscious, surface level of the myth, which was supposed to reflect contemporary life in a realistic manner. Therefore, the division between sentimental and Gothic became more and more pronounced. More and more was the sentimental alone acknowledged as the legitimate mythic expression of the age.

The Light Side of the Myth: Sentimental Tradition

The light aspect of the sentimental/Gothic myth, reflected in the literature of sentiment but implicitly included in antisentimental and Gothic literature as well, is sometimes taken to be complete in itself, a body of symbolism, a code of values and behavior, all reflected to a greater or lesser degree in the literature and manners of its age. In fact, the sentimental tradition by itself is not only incomplete but is also internally flawed in ways that suggest the existence, the completion, of the Gothic. While examining sentimental conventions and the characteristics of the tradition, one is constantly reminded that, although sentimentality represents a cultural effort to repress and deny the darker aspects of human reality, this effort is never wholly successful. The Gothic side of the myth exists just over the border of consciousness; often, indeed, it breaches that border, introducing apparent irrationalities and contradictions within the sentimental tradition itself.

Perhaps the most basic assumption of the sentimental tradition is that feeling is superior to rationality, that the emotions are a better means of knowledge and guide to behavior than is the intellect. The primacy of feeling was asserted apparently as a reaction to the rationalism of the eighteenth century; however, its assertion was also a tacit admission that the rational ideal was impossible of attainment, that emotion existed and informed human behavior, that to attempt the exclusion of emotion from human enterprise not only went against the precepts of contemporary religion (which stressed the importance of personal religious experience, a "spiritual" rather than intellectual affair) but also invited self-delusion and alienation.

The superiority of feeling, of intense personal, emotional knowledge, was repeatedly asserted by the early romantic writers—in conjunction, often, with the idea that the person closest to his own unschooled feelings, like the child, the peasant, the "noble savage," was better able to make correct judgments than those who had learned to distort their native impulses with an excess of rationality. Women, because they were supposed to be less intellectual than men (and were, in any event, usually less burdened with formal education), came to be seen as morally superior because they were thought and encouraged to be more emotionally sensitive. Thus any rational enterprise was thought to gain moral strength from emotional "intuition."

Walter Jackson Bate, analyzing in detail the philosophical development of this regard for feeling, contends that the idea was less wholeheartedly accepted in England than in other countries. Certainly, English writers were to warn against its wholehearted acceptance, but such warnings themselves attest to the wide popularity of the convention, and these writers—Jane Austen is a case in point—accept the convention far more readily than did their Augustan predecessors. The overindulgence of "sensibility" causes trouble for Austen's heroines, but her remedy is *sense,* not cold rationality.

If sense is preferable to rationality, however, neither sense nor sensibility is to be confused with sensuality, especially in England and America. The essential purity of the unschooled individual is one of the basic sentimental assumptions; the association of sensuality with primitive, uncivilized individuals or societies is one of the glaring contradictions of the tradition. An indulgence of purely sensual feeling is always, in sentimental tradition, potentially wrong, and when such feeling is not restrained the result is dangerous, often fatal, to the individual. In *Jane Eyre,* the unchecked sensuality of Bertha Mason has led her to madness; she has become a kind of human beast. Jane herself leaves Rochester in order to avoid the dangers of a too-sensual relationship, and although she rejects the opposite extreme offered by St. John Rivers, she can return to Rochester only when his sensuality has been chastened and cooled—through fire—by blindness. (Barbara Hill Rigney's *Madness and Sexual Politics in the Feminist Novel* presents an interesting discussion of this point.) In *Wuthering Heights,* Catherine and Heathcliff are punished for their lack of sensual restraint; while they remain tremendously attractive to the reader (as they obviously were to Emily Bronte), it is significant that their love "triumphs" only in death.

The distrust of sensual feeling often leads to a complete denial of such feeling; in the most sentimental of literature, even men and children are portrayed as lacking physical appetites of any kind, and women as being virtually bodiless—although their highest aspirations, ironically, are to wifehood and motherhood. This extreme distrust of sensual feeling is hardly to be found in the early romantics, who are famous for their celebrations of physical sensuality. But it is easy to understand how such a distrust arose when one realizes that the Puritan influence upon the myth, combined with the loss of long-standing traditional bulwarks against the incursion of unconscious urges, inspired what amounted to a neurotic fear of pleasure. Without a culturally accepted line between sensual pleasure and sensual license, the individual psyche was threatened with demons of sensuality. Even the great English romantics were not free from these demons, as the almost invariable linking of physical depletion, madness, or death with their celebrations of sensual vitality makes plain.

There was, however, one area of sensual feeling in keeping with the Puritan spirit and the fear of sensuality. As *pleasure* was more and more strongly denied, *suffering* was indulged to a greater and greater extent. Pain, emotional and physical, is in the sentimental code noble and uplifting when accepted in the right spirit—and that right spirit becomes more complex as the myth develops. Certainly, suffering is considered in Christian tradition to be a purging and purifying experience, and sentimental tradition retains this sense of it; Jane's and Rochester's sufferings, for example, make them worthy of each other's love. Also, a villain's intense suffering allows his erstwhile victims (and the reader) a certain satisfaction; in fact, it allows them the same sort of sadistic pleasure the villain has probably enjoyed, while freeing them from moral culpability. For of course it is God or the Universe or fate punishing the offender, rather than the offended person, who may now be forgiving and properly sympathetic. Mrs. Sinclair's horrific death, in *Clarissa,* is a case in point. But Clarissa's own suffering, welcomed by her and lovingly portrayed by Richardson, is prolonged far beyond any doubt that the details of her agony are meant to be relished of and for themselves.

Clarissa was the first in a long line of sentimental heroines whose torments filled pages and packed theaters for generations. Suffering was not only uplifting; it was attractive. And while Clarissa (at least in her own eyes) suffered and died as a Christian heroine, enduring pain with forgiveness and in expectation of heaven, later heroines often suffered for no apparent reason except that frailty, a propensity for pain, constitutional weakness in general, had become components of feminine attractiveness. It is a commonplace that Victorian femininity was most desirable when it was most fragile, in delicate health. And while corsets and weighty layers of clothing no doubt made fits of fainting real enough in many cases, it is another commonplace that ladylike behavior called for the affectation of physical weakness.

Part of the attraction of a woman (or man) in ill health may be the assumed sexual incapacity of such a person. Given a cultural atmosphere in which robust sexuality is seen as threatening, the threat may be removed without explicit avoidance of a sexual relationship if one or the other potential partner is ill. In Bram Stoker's *Dracula,* a Gothic novel in which the sentimental conventions are clearly reflected, the only normal sexual relationship presented is implicitly suggested to be unconsummated until after the major events of the novel have taken place, first because of Jonathan Harker's invalid condition as a result of his experiences in Dracula's castle, and later because his wife has been injured and made "unclean" by the vampire's attack.

The avoidance of sexuality is, however, not the only attraction of the ill or suffering character. Pain itself, and the infliction of pain, are substitutes for—or heighteners of—sexual pleasure. Characters are frequently portrayed as apparently enjoying their suffering. The requisite perils of the typical heroine of melodrama and domestic fiction became so familiar that we know them best through their frequent satirization, but often the satires themselves are ambiguous in tone: to what extent, for example, is Dickens's Miss Havisham a pathetic parody of the Clarissa type, and to what extent a terrifying instance of wronged and suffering femininity, a character exciting to the sensual enjoyment of female degradation?

The substitution of pain for pleasure leads directly, in the sentimental tradition, to the supreme moment of pain, the best and only climax afforded this mode of sensuality—death. As Poe concluded, for ostensibly aesthetic reasons, the most fitting subject for sentimental literature is the death of a beautiful woman. From the long, drawn-out dying of Clarissa Harlow through the deathbed scenes of Little Eva, Beth March, and Melanie Wilkes in three of America's most persistently popular sentimental novels, the literature of sentiment reflects obsessively what Dorothy Van Ghent has termed "a cult...of death" (61). As Leslie Fiedler points out, the eroticism of death in most English and American sentimental literature is remarkably innocent

(265). Only in Heathcliff's terrible passion for the dead Catherine, and in the generally recognized literature of the Gothic tradition, does it approach the frank sadism and necrophilia of Continental literature of the same period, as described by Mario Praz in *The Romantic Agony*. Again, the Puritan tradition, combining the glorification of martyrdom with stark antisensuality, may be responsible for this difference between English and Continental versions of the myth. In any case, while the latter was eventually to influence the English Pre-Raphaelites and "decadent" artists of the late nineteenth century, the relative un-self-consciousness of the former led to a different sort of extreme, a genteel preoccupation with death as satirized by Mark Twain in the Emmeline Grangerford episode of *Huckleberry Finn*.

In line with its middle-class Protestant origins, the morality of the sentimental tradition is unambiguous; in fact it is generally simplistic. Good and evil are easily distinguished, and the point of view is generally moralistic and didactic to some degree. Characters in popular verse, domestic fiction, and melodrama are more often than not presented as flat stereotypes; in serious literature, setting, incident, and character are ostensibly realistic, but true complexity of character or motivation is rare. Indeed, when a morally ambiguous character is found in sentimental fiction, it is probably this characterization more than anything else that makes the fiction memorable. In general, the virtuous character is apparently born virtuous, and temptations put in his or her path seem not so much genuine trials as opportunities for the writer to demonstrate the character's unswerving goodness. A morally bad character, on the other hand (again, exceptions are memorable because they are exceptions) is bad through and through. His or her actions, even physical characteristics, make recognition of this badness (by the reader, at least) easy, and there is little chance of that character's reformation. (Again, the reader is aware of this, though other characters may not immediately accept it; one of the traditional sufferings of the virtuous character is his or her stubborn but vain attempt to "save" the villain.)

Virtue and vice are rewarded or punished more or less publicly, often by material gain or loss. Suffering, as we have seen, is not reserved for a sinful person's punishment, but the *enjoyment* of suffering and death is generally the prerogative of the virtuous: Clarissa enjoys her death, while Mrs. Sinclair exits raving and cursing; Compeyson is ignominiously drowned and left to wash ashore, while Magwitch, although he must be punished for his crimes, is allowed to cheat the gallows and die a peaceful death. It might be noted that the suffering and death of the evil character are usually dreadful if not violent, whereas the death of the virtuous is relatively calm and often picturesque. Outlined in flames, yelling, Bertha Mason dives from the roof of Thornfield Hall; St. John Rivers's death, not yet accomplished, is foreseen in terms of Biblical splendor.

Material gain or loss figures frequently in the sentimental system of reward and punishment. It is a commonplace of melodrama that the villain, who has often exercised material power over the hero or heroine, ends by losing his fortune and being reduced to rags, often having to accept the charity of his erstwhile victim, who has meanwhile risen in fortune. For while genteel poverty is more conducive to virtue than are riches (particularly old, aristocratic wealth), virtue is best shown by material well-being; the sentimental tradition is, indeed, closely allied with the rise of capitalism, which like the myth is rooted in the Calvinist doctrine of election. The poor who remain poor are for the most part inferior types, useful only as they can be bought by the villain or treated kindly by the hero. Those who enjoy their wealth, inherited or earned, are generally deserving of it. And material reward or punishment is often bestowed entirely by coincidence (Jane Eyre's modest inheritance, for example, has no intrinsic connection with the novel's plot), having little to do with the actions of the recipient except in the sense that the character "deserves" it.

The virtues rewarded in the literature of sentiment are those enumerated in Christ's Sermon on the Mount, modified by the Protestant and capitalist work ethic; one need distribute only a reasonable fraction of one's possessions to the poor, and the service of Mammon is not entirely to be avoided. The virtuous person is expected to perform honest work of some kind, and may consider the fowls of the air and lilies of the field at his or her well-earned leisure. These virtues are most often exercised in a domestic setting, for one of the myth's characteristic assumptions is that the family is the most important social unit and marriage and parenthood are the most important relationships. Family loyalties replace national or more distantly fraternal obligations as a central theme, and courtship and love take on an importance unprecedented in English literature.

Symbolically exalted in the literature of the courtly love myth, treated as comedy in Elizabethan, Jacobean, and Reformation drama, the male/female love relationship becomes the dominant theme of the novel, the characteristic sentimental form. And the object of the love relationship is always marriage, whether or not that object is (or can be) attained. The family is sometimes treated as a larger unit than that consisting of one married couple and their children, but always that smaller unit, and the courtship leading to its establishment, are at the heart of the matter.

Fiedler, recognizing Gothic elements as part of the literature of sentiment, correctly asserts that the archetypal lover of the myth is the Seducer, but it must be remembered that the Seducer's ostensible aim is marriage; often he genuinely means (as even Lovelace does) to marry the heroine, and she always supposes that he will—or intends, like Pamela, that he *shall.* But when the Seducer is not a sentimental/Gothic composite of hero and villain, and often even when he is, there is a hero of unmixed character waiting to save the maiden from the Seducer's clutches, or to mourn bitterly if he fails to do so. For the heroine's fall, whether it be through capitulation or capture, often leads to her death and always to her "ruin." Hardy's "Ruined Maid" takes its irony, as many later realistic novels do their realism, from that convention. The composite hero, who functions in both the light and dark sides of the myth, is always a threat to the heroine's virtue (and thus to her life); as such, he is a much more attractive character than the unmixed hero who may or may not be needed to save her from ruin. (St. John Rivers, although he turns out to be deficient in sentimental-heroic qualities, functions as this second type when he first appears in *Jane Eyre,* while the reader is temporarily led to believe that Rochester as Seducer will neither be saved by Jane nor be successful in ruining her.)

As the dualities implicit in the myth cause an increasing tension between the sentimental and the Gothic, sentimental fiction tends to portray the masculine protagonist as two or even more male characters. By the same token, the heroine becomes incapable of containing the contradictory qualities of mythic femininity, and two or more characters (typically the dark and light woman, the lily and rose types of Victorian literature) are needed to express these qualities.

The characters of sentimental literature are primarily defined as they fulfill the roles in which the myth casts them. Men and women are "normal" or "abnormal," virtuous or vicious, as they satisfactorily perform the drama of courtship, marriage, and parenthood, and as they act within the conventions of sensibility designated as *masculine* or *feminine.* (The deviation from supposed sexual norms is generally not seen as abnormality, but rather as vice or a weakness of character—that is, a *moral* weakness—but the labeling of such a deviation as *madness* is quite common, and does not contradict the implied moral culpability of the deviate, since insanity was—and often still is—thought to be the result of a vicious life.) Although sentimental characters are portrayed in what is supposed to be a realistic light—that is, they are put, individually and socially, into situations not unfamiliar and not impossible (however improbable) to the reader—they are in fact as conventionalized by the myopic restrictions of masculinity and femininity as any of the frankly romanticized or allegorical knights and ladies of courtly love tradition. However, the familiarity of situation in sentimental literature, aided by the innately apparent realism of the novel form, persuaded the reader that the portrayal of character was equally realistic. Moreover, the didactic tone, urging readers to perceive sentimental characters as role models, eventually lent a degree of realism to the conventionalized characters as life imitated, or struggled to imitate, art.

The good woman of sentimental tradition is good by nature; she is formed with a fine sensibility, a cheerful disposition, and a natural abhorrence of anything coarse, disproportionate, or blemished. Her intelligence is intuitive rather than analytic; a feminine trait, intuition is not understood to be the result of any sort of reasoning, so that if a woman is correct in her apprehensions no amount of reason can dissuade her. By the same token, if her intuitions fail she is dependent upon masculine reason, just as she is dependent upon masculine passions and strength to support her delicacy and physical weakness. Her purity and sensibility, which twentieth-century readers are apt to find tiresome (or suspiciously artificial), are absolutely indispensable to her femininity. Thus a woman like Mrs. Bennett in *Pride and Prejudice* is still acceptably feminine though selfish and stupid, but her daughter Lydia, coarse and excessively sensual, is deficient in femininity and must be corrected by marriage to a man who we understand will eventually become a cruel master. The difference is between an imbalance of feminine traits, in the mother, and a dangerous appropriation, by the daughter, of properly masculine qualities.

Louisa May Alcott's popular children's book, *Little Women,* illustrates the sentimental conventions of femininity in all its female characters as they approach or fall short of the mark. The purest feminine virtues belong to Beth, the angelic sister whose very hold on physical humanity is so tenuous that, after a short life of uncomplaining service to her family, she drifts softly into death without ever having attained physical womanhood. Beth's apparent asexuality, which is sustained past the end of her teens, is significant: her femininity goes *beyond* the sentimental ideal, in fact, into the realm of the Gothic; she is the Gothic heroine without that figure's traditional antagonist, the Gothic villain or monster, and as the Gothic villain represents the extreme of sexuality, the Gothic heroine represents the opposite extreme. (Interestingly and sadly enough, Beth's counterpart in real life suffered, according to Alcott's biographer Martha Saxon, from an apparent form of anorexia nervosa, one of the symptoms of which is a delay or cessation of menstruation—a psychological and physical rejection of adolescence. The Saxon biography is, in fact, a fascinating attestation to the effects of sentimental conventions on the lives of nineteenth-century women and men.)

Another sister, Amy, exhibits to some degree an imbalance of femininity—a tendency to vanity and pride—but deepens quite inexplicably into womanhood as her time for marriage approaches. The most ideally feminine of the four sisters, in terms of the sentimental side of the myth, is Meg, the eldest; although she is once supposedly tempted into the sort of imbalance typical of Amy's character, she is so bland a "little woman" as to be a remarkably uninteresting literary entity. The least ideally feminine is Jo, whose character is blemished by masculine traits. Jo is treated somewhat ambiguously by Alcott (she based the character on herself); Jo is the most sympathetic and certainly the most interesting of the sisters, and no doubt some degree of antisentimental reflection upon the conventions is intended. But Jo interprets her own desire for independence, her reluctance to put on artificial, "ladylike," airs, to pretend weakness and excessive sensibility—her masculine qualities, in other words—as faults, and so, apparently, does Alcott, at least to some extent. Although most of Jo's masculine strength and rationality is forced upon her by circumstances, and although she attempts to control her "passionate" temper, Alcott punishes her by having the attractive Laurie, Jo's childhood sweetheart, marry Amy, while Jo is married to a much older, fatherly individual whose sexual attractiveness is, to the reader at least, imperceptible. Since neither of these marriages is based on actual events of the Alcott sisters' lives, we are left to assume that the appealingly antisentimental character is, in the novel's terms, judged and punished according to strictly sentimental standards.

Especially interesting is the character of the March girls' mother, a paragon of womanly virtues to her daughters. She remains a character of ideal femininity, revered for her purity and sweetness, her unfailingly cheerful optimism, and her moral strength. Jo, as the masculine daughter, has an interesting relationship with her mother: she feels a special need for her mother's feminine qualities; like many male characters in sentimental fiction, she requires the taming influence of a feminine woman. At the same time, Jo strives to protect the older woman from the world's shocks, a typically masculine function. It is as if the mother, despite her acquaintance with the coarser aspects of life as she goes upon her charitable rounds to the households of the urban poor, is somehow unaware—and must be kept so—of the sordid or distressing truths that the daughter recognizes. For example, she is kept from knowing that Beth's eventually fatal illness was contracted in nursing a sick child of one of Mrs. March's recipient families. Certainly Alcott, whose experience included a period of nursing in an army hospital, did not write euphemistically through any ignorance of harsh realities; again, we must assume that Mrs. March's character, apparently untouched by the things we are told she experiences, is determined entirely by sentimental convention.

The contradictions inherent in this kind of character portrayal are revealing of flaws within the sentimental tradition. If the woman is exposed to the realities of life and death (as she must be to act as an "angel of mercy," one of her requisite roles), the reader must interpret her continuing innocence and delicacy as signs of hypocrisy, unless he can convince himself—as readers who wholly accepted the sentimental myth must have done—that the contradiction does not exist. Victor Frankenstein's description of his mother illustrates the problem:

There was a show of gratitude and worship in [my father's] attachment to my mother...and a desire to be the means of, in some degree, recompensing her for the sorrows she had endured, but which gave inexpressible grace to his behavior to her. Every thing was made to yield to her wishes and her convenience. He strove to shelter her, as a fair exotic is sheltered by the gardener, from every rougher wind, and to surround her with all that could tend to excite pleasurable emotion in her soft and benevolent mind. (33)

It will be my contention that the contradiction implied by Frankenstein is ironically intended (because Carolyn Frankenstein appears elsewhere in the novel as far from "soft"-minded or in need of shelter) to characterize Victor and his family as specifically flawed by the sentimental ideal. To recognize the contradiction, one must remember that a middle-class woman of the late eighteenth or early nineteenth century performed domestic tasks that, even with the help of servants, demanded physical strength and resilience and were unlightened by labor-saving technology. She was also familiar with crude sanitary facilities, with illness and death and the physical details attendant upon both (and was expected to manage these details to a far greater degree than her twentieth-century counterpart). She was certainly familiar, often without having received any instruction in the matter, with the "indelicate" aspects of her own physical nature, including childbearing. A woman's acquaintance with every physical aspect of life was likely to be, in fact, far closer than that of her husband, for she was supposed to attend without his assistance to the management of domestic and charitable activities. But the "delicacy" required of the feminine woman by the sentimental tradition is inconsistent with the realities of women's experience, and these realities were conventionally ignored in the fiction of the period. Thus the fictional feminine woman—and the real woman, too, if she could manage to conform to the requirements of convention—was supposed to know the indelicate facts of life and not to know them at the same time.

The mysterious key that allows this contradiction in a woman's character, although it is never actually acknowledged explicitly, is of course the sexual act, the secret moment in which the most delicate of creatures participates in the most indelicate of realities. Only married women and widows are portrayed as being both knowledgeable and innocent; young virgins are only innocent, while old virgins are unnaturally ignorant, peculiar, often ridiculous. A case in point is Hepzibah Pyncheon of Hawthorne's *House of the Seven Gables,* whose childish innocence, like that of her brother Clifford, is both pathetic and ridiculous. Clifford's unnaturally prolonged childhood is the result of years of imprisonment; Hepzibah's, however, has been preserved through a long life in town along with—and as part of—her virginity.

Another character in the same book, Phoebe Pyncheon, illustrates perfectly the sentimental heroine of the myth's light side; she is the embodiment of sunshine in the sunshine-and-shadows motif of this very consciously crafted romance, and no shadow attaches to her except as she is hauntingly identified with Alice Pyncheon, who, in the daguerreotypist-magician's tale-within-a-tale, is cast entirely into darkness by the mesmerist-magician's art. But a dazzling interplay of sunshine and shadow falls upon the figure of Hawthorne's most famous heroine, Hester Prynn. Branded by her letter and her child as a "scarlet" woman, Hester remains somehow as virginal as Clarissa after Lovelace's rape; unlike Clarissa, however, Hester refuses to suffer. The badges of her adultery become ornaments worn deliberately, and by them she assumes the angel-of-mercy role more truly than the respectable matron or widow of the sentimental myth was ever expected or actually intended to assume it. Hester's scarlet "A" comes to stand for that role as well.

The good man of sentimental myth is generally a great deal easier for twentieth-century readers to accept than the good woman. His qualities are more probable, more human; he is by nature open, passionate, sensual, active, reasonable, strong, where she is demure, chaste, spiritual, passive, intuitive, weak. His positive masculine traits may at times be carried beyond credibility, but he is permitted a sense of healthy honesty as well, which helps to temper his manliness. The fact that his traits are by definition more *human* than hers—the adjectives *manly* and *angelic* define the distinction—makes him less likely to seem artificial; he wears better. Moreover, he is most human when he is, according to the terms of the myth, *excessively* manly, before he has been tamed by marriage.

The point at which we are likely to appreciate the masculine man least is that at which he intersects with his feminine counterpart. Here, we are given to understand, he is saved from the potential excess of masculinity that would dominate his character without the guidance of a good woman (usually his sweetheart or wife, but sometimes his sister or mother), and he is usually portrayed as being both reluctant and eager for her to save him. His reluctance is often understandable, and his eagerness apparently hypocritical at best, since to win her he must be willing to reject not only physical passion but most of the other qualities that have made him seem "natural" to the reader, and he must accept her feminine characteristics, however inexplicable to him, as both natural and superior. As the ideal man must have no feminine qualities of his own, he is dependent upon those of the woman to keep him from excessive masculinity, which would eventually render him brutish and uncivil.

Every masculine sentimental hero, then, is to some extent "Byronic"—excessively masculine, the lover/seducer. The dark or Byronic hero is one who has, for some reason, not yet been saved by feminine intervention; like Rochester, Heathcliff, even Lovelace, he has preserved his untempered masculinity into adulthood, and while he is potentially *ideally* masculine (even Lovelace might be saved, or so the reader must believe), our interest in his character derives from the dramatic struggle between the potential brute and the potential ideal.

This Byronic type is, for obvious reasons, more to be admired in literature than in life, from the point of view of sentimental morality. The masculine ideal is more truly represented by a less interesting character, a man whose potential for excess has already been tamed, often represented by a secondary character, the heroine's father, brother, or the man who will save her from harm or ruin at the hands of the excessively masculine man. Dobbin, in *Vanity Fair,* is this sort of hero, and Thackeray's novel is unconventional partly because Dobbin has a central role while George Osborne, the Byronic hero, exists as a force throughout much of the story only in Amelia's memory. The novel is "without a hero" inasmuch as George Osborne is portrayed as an essentially unattractive character whose heroism is apparent only to Amelia, the sentimentally feminine woman, while Dobbin's lower-class birth and his clumsiness supposedly make him less than heroic. But while it may attempt to debunk the sentimental myth, *Vanity Fair* succeeds better in showing that when one layer of the myth is peeled away, other, deeper layers remain.

The truly bad or perverse woman of sentimental tradition is either passionate, sexually aware and active (though often a bad mother or childless) or perversely willful and intellectual, guided by reason more than intuition and determined to be independent in her own right. The first type is exemplified by Mrs. Sinclair, Bertha Mason, and to a lesser degree by Lydia of *Pride and Prejudice;* the second is illustrated by Becky Sharp of *Vanity Fair* and Scarlett O'Hara of *Gone With the Wind* (both arguably more attractive characters to the modern reader than their more feminine counterparts Amelia and Melanie). Both types are perverse precisely because they have masculine traits. But passionate masculinity, the first type, is much less acceptable in a woman than is intellectual masculinity or a willful, independent spirit. The second type is generally brought low, either by marriage to a cruel and ruthless man or by the desertion of a good man who might have loved her. (Thackeray and Margaret Mitchell both manage, by their manipulation of the characters of Rawdon Crawley and Rhett Butler, to subject their strong-willed heroines to both fates.) The first type of masculine woman, excessively sensual, is more threatening to the mythic standard and is thus often portrayed as being monstrous, like Bertha Mason and Mrs. Sinclair, and punished with horrible suffering and a gruesome death. Lucy Westenra, in *Dracula,* is revealed as an example of this type—she has enjoyed and encouraged the courtship of three young men at once and reacts sensuously to Dracula's seduction—when she becomes a vampire who preys on young children and is eventually destroyed by her three erstwhile suitors.

The sentimental tradition does not recognize an excess of femininity as it does of masculinity. Some women are bad, in terms of the myth, because their feminine traits are unbalanced; they are too proud or vain with too little kindness or humility (Mrs. Bennett of *Pride and Prejudice,* Blanche Ingram and Georgiana Reed of *Jane Eyre* are examples of such imbalance); or they are simply old and unmarried and are punished or ridiculed accordingly, though never so severely punished as the masculine woman. Pride and vanity are actually desirable feminine traits, when properly balanced, and purity is expected to be fruitful. But femininity is not supposed to be tempered or reduced by masculinity, as masculinity is tempered or reduced by femininity; it is simply meant to be protected and supported in the union sought by the myth.

In one sense, however, an excess of femininity does appear in expressions of sentimentality—but when it appears it is an unconscious acknowledgment of the Gothic. Clarissa Harlowe, Helen Burns of *Jane Eyre,* Amelia Sedley, Melanie Wilkes of *Gone With the Wind,* Beth March, in fact all the suffering and dying sentimental heroines, are excessively feminine women; their femininity is too pure for them to accept the necessary union with masculinity. This is, in fact, often said directly of such characters, who are sentimentally judged as being too angelic to continue in an earthly existence. In fact their sufferings and deaths are the punishments visited upon them for their excess. However, the light side of the myth does not acknowledge either the nature of their fault or the nature of their fate; they are praised for their pure femininity, which is extolled as the highest good for which a woman may strive, and their pain is seen as a kind of reward. Amelia Sedley, for example, sees her own unreasonably prolonged mourning for George Osborne as a virtue; Thackeray is able to show its destructive effects, at the end of the novel, in an ironic light precisely because the reader will have expected a conventionally happy ending for this sentimentally virtuous character. We shall see, when we examine the Gothic side of the myth, that femininity, while it is always to be praised, is always to be punished.

The bad man of sentimental myth is, infrequently, a perversely feminine man. He may be oversensitive and thus lacking in courage or strength of will (Arthur Dimmesdale of *The Scarlet Letter*); he may be vain, and thus ridiculous (Joseph Sedley of *Vanity Fair*). There is no masculine strength outside of himself for an adult man to draw upon, if he is insufficiently masculine himself—although he may sometimes be partly redeemed by his dependence upon God. In *Dracula,* the very existence and proximity of the excessively masculine Count seem to drain masculinity from the hero, Jonathan Harker, who reacts effeminately (faints, becomes ill) and begins to depend for masculine strength upon Dr. Van Helsing; Van Helsing himself, a strong father-figure, must support his own threatened masculinity with the cross, the host, and other symbols of masculinity. But neither of these sentimental characters, within a very Gothic novel, is actually feminine—as I will argue for Victor Frankenstein, their masculine strengths have simply been depleted by the magnetism of the excessively masculine monster, and their apparently feminine behavior actually reflects this depletion rather than any "positive" feminine trait. Thus Van Helsing must rely on symbolism that is itself (as in *The Monk* and *Melmoth the Wanderer*) generally seen as antithetical to sentimentality, while Harker is unable without Van Helsing's support to perform his masculine role of protecting and supporting the feminine characters.

The depleted male is almost invariably a Gothic figure, for he is depleted by the projection of unacceptable qualities, including excessive masculinity; in the sentimental tradition an absence of these qualities is a purportedly desirable state, achieved through taming feminine influence but seldom actually shown (as the tamed Rochester is not actually shown in *Jane Eyre*). In fact, it is difficult to find, in the literature of sentiment, a man who is perversely feminine to the degree that Bertha Mason, for example, is a perversely masculine woman—perhaps because this kind of perceived distortion of normality has always been too frightening to be consciously admitted by the sentimental tradition, since the sentimental point of view must recognize unconsciously that both masculinity and femininity as it defines them are themselves distortions of actual human nature and behavior. Most bad or potentially bad men to be found in sentimental literature are either unbalanced in their masculinity (coldly intellectual, without human passions, as St. John Rivers appears at first in *Jane Eyre,* or cruel and dishonest in their dealings with other men, as Rawdon Crawley is initially portrayed, becoming more balanced as he is required to punish Becky, in *Vanity Fair*) or they are excessively masculine, untamed and perhaps untamable, in which case they retain a degree of attractiveness despite the punishment eventually meted out to them.

Leslie Fiedler argues that, although the sentimental novel began its career (in Richardson's novels) as a male production, it soon became an essentially female statement to whose terms male authors and men in general acquiesced. However, as Kate Millet and other feminist writers have successfully demonstrated, it can hardly be supposed that an unbiased female perspective came to hold sway in this segment of a culture otherwise dominated by men— even if there were not overwhelming evidence in the myth itself that it is finally an expression of hostility toward femininity. A genuinely female point of view (such as that expressed, for example, by Mary Wollstonecraft) must have been developed only rarely within the culture dominated by the sentimental myth; even Jane Austen, the Brontes, and other strong women writers, as has been seen in the case of Louisa May Alcott, exhibit various degrees of ambiguity in the portrayal of male and female characters. And it is almost always in the works of women that we find the antisentimental element expressed most strongly, recognizing or partly recognizing sentimentality as a set of conventions and playing off those conventions for literary interest or realism.

Thus one of the few male characters to exhibit perversely feminine traits, and to be rewarded by a typically feminine fate, appears in Charlotte Bronte's *Jane Eyre*: St. John Rivers, as he is revealed in the second part of his characterization, is not really the coldly dispassionate figure he seems at first, nor is he the apparently feminine, actually depleted, victim of the Gothic tradition; he is, in fact, an excessively *feminine* character, whose passivity, lack of physical passion, human charity, and suggested masochism (all positive feminine traits as seen by the myth) represent for Jane the temptation to excessive femininity that she successfully resists. Like Helen Burns, earlier in the novel, he is too pure to maintain physical existence, and although both characters attract the antisentimental heroine to a degree, she avoids the fatal urge to pure femininity as deftly as she avoids its polar opposite, excessive masculinity, represented by the untamed Rochester and Bertha Mason.

The differences between masculinity and femininity, standing at the heart of the sentimental tradition, are exceptionally complex. Femininity seems to be a composite of two *kinds* of trait: first, those civilized and civilizing virtues that men have seen as necessary for the maintenance of a comfortable and well-regulated society, but that they reject in themselves as weaknesses (such as tenderheartedness and piety) or signs of impracticality (intuition, aestheticism) inconsistent with the economic and social dominance also demanded by the myth; and, second, those real vices or weaknesses that are actually found in both sexes but are unacceptable to the male point of view as masculine traits (vanity, duplicitousness, for example). Masculinity, on the other hand, is composed of those traits that must be admired as strengths but that are recognized as dangerous unless controlled (such as aggressiveness, passion, and willfulness) as well as virtues that may be found in persons of either sex (intellectual ability, physical strength, and skill) but are traditionally discouraged in females within a male-dominated culture.

Because the point of view of the sentimental tradition is basically male (although it is accepted by men and women alike), the tradition warns against but scarcely despises excessive or uncontrolled masculinity, idealizes but resists tamed masculinity, and refuses even to admit the existence of feminine traits, as it has defined them, in men. Femininity, to this point of view, is at once admirable and despicable, loved and hated, desirable and repellent by turns, for this label is in reality a catchall for a whole collection of disparate traits that are, to the dominant male point of view, necessary but irreconcilable with human strength—including traits of men themselves that they do not wish to acknowledge, and conventions of contemporary society that they value but find stifling. No wonder that women came to be viewed, often, as enigmas—especially when real women attempted or were forced to conform to the pattern imposed mythically upon their sex.

Although the myth attempts to make masculine and feminine inseparable from male and female, the two sets of terms are really neither identical nor interchangeable. The arbitrariness of the sentimental conventions of masculinity and femininity is made clear in the work of modern writers like Jean Genet, as Kate Millet has demonstrated in *Sexual Politics.* But it is implicit in many less obviously sexual and transsexual situations throughout the literature, especially the Gothic literature, of the myth.

A final aspect of sentimental masculinity and femininity is their interdependence. Each quality requires the other, either to temper and restrain it or to support it, even though a mixture of the two within an individual of either sex is abhorrent. Thus a relationship between a masculine man and a feminine woman, a union in which the two qualities may interact, is necessary. But the nature of this interaction is reflected differently by the light and dark sides of the myth. In the light aspect, the relationship is one of love, of gentle restraint and softening on the one side, strength and protection on the other. The dark aspect of the myth reveals a relationship of pursuit and avoidance, of fear, punishment, attempted possession, and a retaliatory violence that turns masculinity monstrous and deprives femininity of its life. The two opposing forces, expressed in terms of gender and identified with the participants in a sexual relationship, are finally too polarized—and the repressed, unconscious elements too strong—to be resolved by the artificial resolution attempted more and more compulsively in the sentimental tradition. Contradictions between human nature as it wished to see itself and as it really existed were too powerful to be without real effect.

Reality as it is portrayed in the sentimental tradition has so little in common with the facts of life in the world it was supposed to reflect that it is difficult to grasp how anyone managed to accept its purported realism. It seems impossible that sensibility, Christian morality, and feminine superiority could actually have been exalted in myth—that is to say, could have been taken seriously—by people aware in the least of the realities of nineteenth-century life. One is troubled by the apparent hypocrisy of writers who were obviously aware of these realities and yet insisted upon the truth of the sentimental vision; still, one hesitates to accuse such writers—Dickens, for example—of conscious hypocrisy. The fact is that intrinsic contradictions existed within the sentimental tradition itself, as well as between it and the actual world. Even within the myth, the celebration of marriage and love runs headlong into the denial of sexuality; the preoccupation with death negates the exaltation of birth, life, sunshine and happy endings; the homage paid to femininity cannot conceal the fact that female characters are consistently if not consciously made the objects of hostility and violence. Such internal contradictions suggest, rather than hypocrisy, a widespread split in cultural consciousness, marked by the almost compulsive insistence on adherence to one side of the cultural myth and the more and more disturbing expression, in veiled, Gothic terms, of the other.

What, then, were the implications of the sentimental tradition for those to whom it represented a way of viewing reality? Most important, of course, was the new *kind* of reality it represented; whereas the courtly love myth had allowed its adherents to distinguish clearly between their ordinary lives and the symbolic truths of the myth, those who lived surrounded by the atmosphere of sentimental contradictions had no such means of escape. Because the characters and attitudes of sentimental tradition were supposed to be not only real but *actual,* its conventions became a code for ordinary behavior. Men were expected to conduct their relationships with parents, sweethearts, wives, and children according to this code, and to suppress their femininity at all costs while at the same time curbing their acknowledged (and thus cultivated) but undesirable masculine passions. Women were expected to exhibit only those traits that the myth allowed as feminine, and in fact whole generations of women were so affected by these conventions that they lived their lives in the belief that they actually possessed these—and only these— traits.

The resultant social and psychological disturbances, the pathetic Victorian case histories, are well documented. But while the light side of the sentimental/Gothic myth was thus enacted, both at the expense of those individuals who could not manage to comply with its rules and at the less obvious, but just as real, expense of those who could, the dark or Gothic side was also exhibited in actual human behavior. One must remember that, in a culture that longed for sweetness and light, the commonplaces of life included madness, cruel sexual perversions, crime as violent and as casually committed as any twentieth-century crime, and the nearly unbelievable conditions of squalor and suffering in those human communities that the sentimental tradition allowed its adherents to ignore. The Irish famine of the middle nineteenth century stemmed from and produced conditions that were more shocking even than those of Dickens's London; the fictional Mr. Hyde was no more an exaggeration of human reality than was his actual contemporary, Jack the Ripper.

The myth, in its light aspect, fulfilled a purpose at once consciously didactic and psychologically necessary to readers of sentimental fiction, who were participants in the mythos. By portraying certain feelings, modes of behavior, and values as desirable and others as unacceptable, it educated members of the middle classes to take their proper places within the cultural system. It helped to ensure the maintenance of that system by the imposition of feelings, modes of behavior, and values that were highly artificial and by means of which a divided and self-contradictory morality might be kept in control. The sentimental tradition thus served to order, didactically, a cultural situation that required a good deal of artificiality on the part of those living within it. At the same time, the light side of the myth reinforced itself psychologically by assuring its participants that it was a true and undistorted reflection of reality, that its portrayal of human nature was not only morally correct but also physically and psychologically accurate. Such assurance was no doubt distressing to the individual who felt the portrayal to be inaccurate in his or her case, but this probably happened relatively infrequently, as such a deeply pervasive cultural mythos does actually determine and condition many of the attitudes and emotions an individual perceives as his own; in any case, a suspicion of his own abnormality is balanced, for the individual, by the security that a strong code of normality provides.

The light side of the myth fulfilled another purpose as well. Its contradictions, because it did not acknowledge them as contradictions, also served in some degree to afford a release of unconscious impulses that the myth's participants did not wish to recognize. For example, by exercising feminine traits mythically assigned to her, a woman was able to burden men with responsibility, frustration, and guilt without ever being consciously aware that she was doing so; by the same token, in shielding women from expressions of passion in a conscious regard for their mythic delicacy, men could in effect withhold sexual pleasure from them, expressing hostility without having to recognize or acknowledge it as such. Men could, in fact, actually withhold from women the full range of adult experience in the belief that to do so was their masculine responsibility. For a more effective release of hostile impulses, however, the Gothic side of the myth was necessary.

The Dark Side of the Myth: The Gothic Mirror

The sentimental/Gothic myth, in its light and dark aspects, represents a desperate struggle to control the unconscious forces of human emotion, to make psychic reality consistent with practical, ostensibly rational, human purposes. The light side of the myth, by straining to disguise and if possible to deny the existence of unacceptable and unconscious truths, recognizes their deep-rootedness and their strength. The power of these truths erupts, in the Gothic, in strange and terrible ways.

Criticism has wrestled with definitions of the Gothic, and with classification of certain works or sections of works as Gothic in nature, for at least as long as what Mario Praz, in *The Romantic Agony,* calls "terror-romanticism" or the "tale of terror" has been recognized as a serious and psychologically significant literary phenomenon. If, as Thomas Thornburg writes, "the Gothic in fiction is the metaphor of the demonic" (19), then the Gothic may be seen throughout all fiction that attempts to portray not only the acceptable, respectable, conscious ideals of the human race but also those human truths that are rejected, denegrated, cast into darkness, repressed within the unconscious. No doubt some human experiences—chaos, murder, despair, unholy madness, death, and the dead—are always, by the nature of civilization, in eclipse. But with these become allied, at various times, ideas and experiences that have been—or will be—at other times regarded as bathed in light. The study of the natural world, once denegrated as a demonic pursuit, is to most twentieth-century Western minds the epitome of enlightenment, while the medieval suppression and persecution of science have become figures of the demonic.

The shadow of any culture is revealing of that culture's character (as, according to Jungian psychology, the shadow or demonic portion of the individual's personality is a compensatory composite of traits left out of the ego-personality). Thus, when in the middle eighteenth century the world view examined above as the sentimental tradition emerged to represent a segment of Western culture as it came increasingly to regard itself, it was complete with its dark or demonic side. The term "Gothic literature" is generally understood to refer to "the sudden...surge which took its impetus from Walpole's *Otranto"* (Thornburg, 19), whose ebb and flow are still discernible in twentieth-century literature. Identification of the Gothic with the sentimental tradition, as the reversal or dark completion of overt sentimentality, resolves many of the critical problems of definition, of linguistic or cultural and historical locus, of form, and of relationship to other literature.

The Gothic in this sense is expressed in various modes of Western art, but most often in those forms and genres that flourished in the latter half of the eighteenth century and throughout the nineteenth century. It is most characteristically to be found in fiction, specifically in the prose romance and novel. Like the sentimental tradition, it is a middle-class phenomenon, strongest where the Puritan influence is most pronounced. It has its beginnings in political, economic, religious and societal changes that called for mythic recognition, but is rooted in earlier mythic literature whose place it took. Like the light side of the myth, the Gothic is incomplete in itself, self-contradictory, unbalanced.

The Gothic in fiction is concerned with elements that have probably always been regarded as demonic: chaos, murder, despair, death, and the dead. It is also, because of the nature of the divided myth, about those things that the overt side of the myth attempts to deny: violence, lawlessness, the undomesticated individual, the unconscious, the triumph of evil in human affairs, the possibility and the reality of spiritual possession (holy madness as well as unholy madness), the wilderness, sensuality, sexual passion. The Gothic villain is everything the sentimental hero has rejected; the Gothic dark woman or villainess is everything the sentimental heroine must not be. The hero and heroine of Gothic literature are good sentimental characters, carried to the inevitable extremes sentimental literature dares not show—the tamed masculine hero becomes the depleted male victim, the pure sentimental heroine becomes the dying maiden, the murdered bride. And, like the characters in sentimental and Gothic literature, the very settings of fiction reveal a division of what was a multidimensional whole in earlier mythic literature. For example, the castle of the courtly love myth becomes, in the later divided myth, the country house of sentimental literature and the nightmarish and labyrinthine ruin of the Gothic tale. The enchanted forest becomes, on one hand, the carefully cultivated garden, and on the other the shadowy wilderness. Thus concepts and figures whose light and dark aspects were once combined in the literature of myth become divided, their fragmented parts standing alone and at odds with each other. And the Gothic figures are almost always evocative of terror.

The older mythic concepts and figures are distinguished in several ways from those of the divided myth. First, they are somehow removed from the ordinary lives of those for whom the older myths were current. They are distant in time or location (just as "long ago and far away" is a comforting introduction to fairy tales, so it is for any mythic literature), in mode of existence (supernatural or magical), and usually in literary form (the epic or verse romance). In addition, the mythic power of these figures is universalized; as "dogmatic archetypes" in Jungian terms, their origins in the individual human psyche are neither immediate nor threatening. Finally, these figures are almost always ambiguous in character, combining or alternating light and dark archetypal aspects.

With the movement into sentimental/Gothic myth, each figure is divided into two, both incomplete and in opposition to each other. The first is a safe, consciously acceptable component, the second a figure containing all unacceptable or threatening aspects of the character or concept. In neither the sentimental nor the Gothic incarnation is the earlier distance provided. The sentimental figure is supposed to be realistic and contemporary or nearly so, existing in a familiar setting or one that the reader might encounter within the ordinary course of his or her life (as on a trip to the country or city, or a foreign tour). There is nothing supernatural about the sentimental figure; in fact, as has been noted, the reader is encouraged to believe that the most unnatural sentimental behavior is normal, is indeed to be emulated. There is, at least purportedly, nothing ambiguous in the morality or attractiveness of the sentimental figure. And finally, the most common sentimental literary form—the novel—typically eliminates distance between the reader and fictional events and characters.

The Gothic figure may at first seem, by contrast, abnormal, even in some cases supernatural, and it is often apparently removed in time and or location from the familiar world of the reader. But in every case the Gothic figure is distinguished by its lack of *dependable* distance—by the threat it poses to sentimental characters with whom readers are expected to identify. Jonathan Harker's journey into Dracula's country is recorded in a typical tourist's journal; the young heroes and heroines of *The Monk, Melmoth the Wanderer,* and Ann Radcliffe's novels are in most ways indistinguishable from their counterparts in sentimental literature. This lack of distance is necessary to make the Gothic effective; its terror must threaten the normal world of sentiment. In addition, the Gothic figures are not members of dogmatic archetypes; they may, to modern readers, have acquired the familiarity of the traditional, but in the context of the time in which they first appeared they emanate from and speak directly to the unconscious of the individual writer and the contemporary reader. They are as immediate as nightmares, and there is no available body of dogma or ceremony to counter their threat. Moreover, the ambiguity of the earlier figure, its combination of dark and light aspects, persists only partly and in a dangerously altered fashion in the Gothic. Because the figure is immediate for contemporary readers, its darkness is threatening and its immorality emphatic; at the same time, its emotional attractiveness is generally intense.

Because the division between masculinity and femininity is basic to the sentimental/Gothic myth, sentimental characters are portrayed as good or bad as they approach or fall short of the standards of these abstractions. On the Gothic side of the myth the same division is central, but characters are distorted, often perverse reflections of their sentimental counterparts. The good, i.e., feminine, woman, already frail and oversensitive in her sentimental manifestation, becomes in the Gothic unmistakably a victim, a neurasthenic creature whose very fragility and spirituality are the source of her attraction. She often seems actively to seek pain, and pain is certainly her lot. She is most feminine at the moment of her death. Thus Clarissa is revealed as a Gothic heroine. Thus Lucy Westenra, perversely masculine before her first encounter with the vampire and after her transformation, becomes most appealing to the men who love her as she approaches perfect femininity during the period before her false death as Dracula's victim. Madeleine Usher, like many of Poe's female characters, is the epitome of the Gothic feminine woman because of the bizarre illness that allows her to be both dying and apparently dead at once.

The good man of sentimental myth, because his natural (excessive) masculinity has been tamed by feminine influence, becomes in his own way a victim in his Gothic manifestation. Generally he escapes the villain's devastations himself (as Jonathan Harker narrowly does), but he is depicted as a helpless onlooker whose heroic actions are useless or, ironically, actually harmful (as Harker, having escaped his domestication long enough to bring evil in the shape of Dracula into his own world, blunders into allowing the monster access to his friends and wife). As has been remarked, the very presence of Gothic evil apparently depletes the sentimental hero of the qualities needed to combat that evil.

The Gothic villain and villainess are familiar to us from the sentimental tradition: Lovelace, Mrs. Sinclair, Bertha Mason, even to a degree the unchastened Rochester—uncontrolled, passionate characters—are all Gothic in nature. They are moved to action by an inner force that the sentimental myth has rejected: sensual passion, a masculine urge that always manifests itself as cruelty and violence. Insofar as their excessive masculinity may be tempered, they may be—or may appear to be—redeemable. But the difference between these and the more commonly acknowledged monsters of Gothic evil—Ambrosio, Matilda, Melmoth, Frankenstein's Monster, the undead Lucy Westenra, even Dracula himself—is one of degree, not of kind. And it is a mark of the Gothic that Rochester *may* become Lovelace, that Lucy in life, whose overpassionate nature seems scarcely to represent excessive masculinity at first, may and does become a terrifying monster. Though the sentimental world pretends that the Gothic world does not exist, the looking glass that divides the two may be entered at any moment.

The figure of the looking glass is an appropriate one. The Gothic is, in some respects, a direct reversal of the sentimental tradition. Where the sentimental seeks to reassure us that innocence and purity are blessed, that right and wrong are easily distinguishable, that conformity to its code of moral and social behavior will be rewarded, the Gothic refutes such assurance. The pure of heart, the meek and innocent, are natural prey to Gothic monsters. Evil appears in the guise of good and cannot be recognized, except by accident, even by the most virtuous. In the dark world of the Gothic, boundaries are invisible; anything can happen. Virtue is punished and vice rewarded. If, at the end of the tale, the sentimental code is suddenly reinstated, we sense that its reinstatement is arbitrary or impotent. Victor Frankenstein and his family and friends are dead; the Monster survives. Dracula escapes into the mist of sunset, between the very words of Stoker's novel. Ambrosio is cast howling into the pit, but the fiends who put him there are free. The Gothic reverses and refutes the sentimental.

Even more frequently, the Gothic undermines the sentimental by taking it to the boundary it approaches but will not cross, showing that its inevitable direction is toward darkness. The Gothic completes the sentimental, undoes its knotty contradictions, reflects it in a mirror whose distortions mimic its own. For example, the sentimental tradition rejects both cold reason and warm passion as excessively masculine traits, proposing in their place *sensibility,* an essentially feminine trait supposedly composed of neither reason nor passion but instead of a kind of idealized, pure emotion innate in feminine women and necessary to the tempering of masculinity in men. In the Gothic mirror, pure feminine sensibility is clearly revealed as another form of sensuality, complementary to aggressive masculine passion. While the sentimental tradition insists that the union of these two traits produces a balanced masculine-feminine relationship, moralizing and taming on one side, protective and supportive on the other, the Gothic allows the two sides to follow their complementary paths to sensuality to the destructive excess of both.

The Gothic heroine is a passive, pallid creature not so much because she is frail and helpless but because she is, necessarily, so blind to the dangers she courts that we suspect her blindness is deliberate—as, indeed, like any unconsciously motivated behavior, it is. Walpole's unfortunate characters in *The Castle of Otranto,* Ann Radcliffe's imperiled heroines, all sentimental victims in their Gothic manifestations, make wrong choices and encounter disaster at every turn; Mina Murray and Lucy Westenra ignore or forget until too late the signs of Lucy's physical and spiritual peril that are obvious to them even if they do not know what the signs mean; Elizabeth Lavenza subtly taunts Victor Frankenstein, insisting upon the marriage he is apparently reluctant to celebrate, and then fails to see what she of all people should be most able to see—the madness that impels him to wander through the halls on their wedding night while she waits passively for the Monster to appear in her bedroom. In fact, because modern readers are less inclined than their eighteenth- and nineteenth-century counterparts to admire feminine passivity for its own sake, we are in a better position than they were to realize that the extreme passivity of the Gothic heroine is itself monstrous, for the Gothic reveals this aspect of sentimental femininity as a deliberate pursuit of the passive enjoyment of pain. And from the points of view of both the passive and active participants, the ultimate attraction of passive femininity is the beauty of death (the beauty that Jane Eyre resists twice in her rejection of Helen Burns's fate and of St. John Rivers's invitation to join him in martyrdom) and of the dead (the terrible feminine beauty to which the barely perceptible signs of decay have lent their charms, so often and so lovingly described by Poe).

As revealed by the Gothic, the natural direction of feeling, once chosen in preference to reason, is toward total sensuality; and when sensuality is not directed toward the pursuit of pleasure (Ambrosio's downfall in *The Monk*), it is directed toward the pursuit of pain. Both, finally, are directed toward death, for the excess of pleasure and the excess of pain both end in sterility, the life-in-death of the vampire and the death-in-life of the vampire's victim. Either the jungle or the wasteland, the heart of darkness or the white wilderness of the Arctic, is Gothic territory. Although the sentimental tradition seeks to establish itself firmly in temperate climates, wilderness and wasteland encroach upon it from every side.

The sentimental insistence upon middle-class virtue and the virtuousness of the middle class is likewise exposed in the Gothic as a self-deceptive and finally powerless stance. Gothic villains—for example, Lovelace, Radcliffe's

Montoni, Count Dracula—are aristocrats, and their aristocratic charm invariably impresses the middle-class characters who will be their victims. Again, the Gothic does not deny the sentimental proposition—that money (old, unearned, undeserved money) and the power of the feudal lord are evil—but it refuses to agree that upright bourgeois gentility or proud poverty can prevail against them. Dracula, after having literally drained his own fiefdom, uses his title and arrogance of power to acquire new territory in England. And but for the sentimental good fortune of Lucy's friends (for it is not Lucy's good fortune) in her having had a rich and titled lover—who, being earnestly middle-class in his adherence to the sentimental code, deserves his fortune—Dracula would soon rule in his adopted land as well, for "the blood is the life," as Dracula's minion Renfield reminds anyone who will listen. And Mina innocently thanks goodness for Lord Godalming's title and money, forgetting that the same power, used not for God or alming but to grease the wheels of bureaucracy and to impress and charm her own middle-class husband and his employers into providing maps and deeds, admitted the enemy into her country in the first place.

The villain's sycophants and accomplices are likely to be from the other end of the social and economic scale. In the sentimental tradition the poor are blessed sufferers, recipients of middle-class charity, whose actual condition is generally softened in deference to genteel sensibilities—and, in fact, is probably genuinely unknown by most members of the dominant culture for whom sentimental conventions represent reality. The Gothic brings this sentimentally suppressed awareness of poverty into light, recognizing need and ignorance as monstrous twin forces that welcome evil's advances. In Dickens's *Bleak House* and *Great Expectations,* the relationship between evil and socioeconomic class is illustrated by the characters Grandfather Smallweed and Magwitch. The characters with whom these two ally themselves, for material gain, are themselves aristocrats only by association, but the association in both cases is unmistakable and ironic: Compeyson, in *Great Expectations,* pretends to be a gentleman in his courtship of Miss Havisham; the lawyer Tulkinghorn, in *Bleak House,* is a vampire who preys on his clients and their adversaries alike, and is the actual controller of the power of the aristocrats who retain him. Magwitch's first encounter with Compeyson, in which both parties recognize the potential gain to be had from their association, bears an eerie resemblance to the master-servant relationship between Dracula and the madman Renfield.

The middle-class sentimental tradition has a perilous road to go, between the threat of the vengeful aristocracy on one hand and a guilty awareness of its own downtrodden victims on the other. Again, the Gothic, gluttonous for the wealth both disdained and jealously guarded by contradictory sentimental conventions, encroaches from both sides.

Even narrower and certainly more winding is the way by which sentimental tradition attempts to reconcile its various demanding conventions regarding romantic love (absolutely necessary for the happiness and completion of the individual), marriage and the family (the only acceptable outcome of romantic love, highly restricted by codes of class and property), and sexual passion (unacceptable in a good man, unthinkable in a good woman). Obviously, the ideal situation can be achieved only when a number of highly unlikely factors occur in conjunction. A romantic attachment must be formed between a man and woman who are socially and economically acceptable to each other's families, without there being any question of the attraction's dependence upon mere convention or convenience; that is, what is essentially an arrangement of economic practicality must appear, even to the participants, to be a love match. The beloved must be selected from among an extremely narrow range of acquaintances; the attachment must be formed sometime during a span of fewer than ten (probably fewer than five) years of the woman's life; and the courtship must be conducted within a structured behavioral code that allows for no private and little if any direct communication between the two individuals.

Furthermore, the relationship must be formed between two individuals whose social conditioning has ensured that they have little experience or understanding in common, and whose code of behavior demands that they feign an even more exaggerated degree of difference between them than actually exists. The man must wait until the right economic moment (which is likely to be ten or more years beyond his legal majority and may be twenty or more years after his attainment of sexual maturity) to marry, making either a long engagement or a wide difference in age probable. Neither party may engage in premarital sexual activity, and neither must admit to sexual desires or frustrations while both must exhibit warm personal affection. During the courtship and betrothal periods, both must play the required roles of the sentimental code as well as they are able, convincing each other and themselves that the roles are natural.

Although the frequency of such situations' occurrence in sentimental fiction strains the credulity of modern readers, this state of affairs is not, for the sentimental tradition, supposed to be improbable or even supposed to be *ideal* (thus allowing for some stretching of the rules for ordinary human beings); it is actually expected of every normal couple. Each individual, moreover, is supposed to believe that the almost inhuman requirements of the code are imposed in the name of love, that to fail to meet them is to dishonor and disappoint the beloved. One need only read Byron's letters written during his courtship of Miss Milbanke to be struck by the damage this code imposed on the integrity of both individuals; the surprise is not that this particular relationship was destroyed, but that many such relationships did, at least outwardly, survive. Even if we concede that the emotional requirements and satisfactions of individuals are to a great extent determined by cultural expectations, still the emotional dangers of such extremely contradictory requirements as these must be apparent. The Gothic reveals these dangers in its monstrous parodies of love and marriage.

The basic duality that is the nature of the Gothic is reflected in the two most frequently encountered forms of sexuality portrayed in Gothic literature: sado-masochism and incest. Both forms function figuratively as threats to the normal sentimental love relationship; each represents one extreme of the contradictory convention of sentimental love, and thus each represents the dangerous completion of the mythic concept delineated but not examined in the conscious sentimental code.

The theme of incest is widely recognized as being common in Gothic literature. Morton Kaplan and Robert Kloss, psychoanalytic critics whose orthodox Freudian views make this theme of special interest and importance to their criticism, discuss the subject, as well as the attention given it by other scholars of the Gothic, at length in their study *The Unspoken Motive*. The relevance of incest as a key to the relationship between the sentimental tradition and Gothic literature is apparent not only because the subject is so common in Gothic manifestations of the myth, but also because, as will be recalled, the entire sentimental/Gothic myth is rooted in the courtly love tradition, in which perception of the Lady is necessarily colored by the incestuous nature of her suitor's relationship with her.

Kaplan and Kloss contend that incest is basic to the nature and meaning of the Gothic, that the incestuous desires expressed in this literature are directly responsible for its atmosphere of terror and also for the sado-masochism that has seemed to some readers to be the central Gothic figure for sexual relationships. Kaplan and Kloss also relate the Gothic incest theme to the doppelgänger motif frequently found in Gothic literature, as both concepts are related to the feeling of hostility manifested by the oedipal child and the adult who has not resolved his childish incestuous conflicts. In their traditionally Freudian view, not only outwardly innocent relationships involving parent and child (or substitute figures), but also overtly or covertly incestuous relationships between brother and sister (or substitute figures), are in the Gothic "melodrama" covert expressions of the oedipal desire for the opposite-sex parent.

Because this desire necessarily involves hostility toward both parents, these writers say, it arouses feelings of guilt and anxiety and must be resolved by the child. The masking of both desire and hostility, in the Gothic, is in this view necessary for the reader to face the real meaning of the story. The atmosphere of terror (masking feelings of gratification and revulsion), the substitute relationships (including brother-sister incest, which is not as threatening as the oedipal desire because it does not involve murderous wishes toward the parent), and also the doppelgänger, are all forms of masking employed in the Gothic, according to Kaplan and Kloss. The doppelgänger permits the protagonist—the reader's surrogate—to behave toward the parent or the parent substitute in several different ways at once; of the pair or set of characters representing the protagonist, one may act as a devoted child, another as a lover, and another may exercise violence or hostility toward the parent figure. Still another form of masking, say Kaplan and Kloss, is the substitution of apparently natural illnesses and accident for actual violence performed by one of the protagonist doppelgängers.

This analysis of the connection between the themes of incest, sado-masochism (the "punishment" of the beloved, by which ambivalent feelings are expressed), and the doppelgänger provides a valuable insight into Gothic literature. However, by interpreting all symbols of incest—and all overtly portrayed incestuous relationships—as having immediate reference to the protagonist's oedipal desires, Kaplan and Kloss fail to explain fully the significance of incest as a figurative device of the Gothic. Several peculiarities of Gothic literature suggest that the matter is even more complicated than their discussion suggests. It has already been seen that oedipal feelings were strongly expressed in the literature of courtly love. Yet incest as it appears in Gothic literature, both overtly and covertly, is treated differently in several important respects, and the differences suggest that something more than the expression of oedipal emotions, though no doubt related to such emotions, is implied.

In courtly love literature, the male protagonist was characteristically involved with a woman who, by age or station (and often by implied association with the Virgin), could readily be identified as a mother-figure. Simply stated, the explicit adultery or desire to commit adultery so common to this myth stands for incest or the desire to commit incest. The Lady is married, if not to her lover's own feudal lord, at least to a man older or of higher rank than the suitor, a mythic representation of the father. The winning of the Lady may require a battle with her husband, or it may involve a disloyalty to him that renders the lover incapable, because unworthy, of successfully completing his quest—as, for example, Lancelot's disloyalty to Arthur through his adultery with Guinevere affects his performance of the Grail quest. The basic story is of the son's desire to possess his mother. The myth of courtly love is related, in this sense, to the "year's king" ritual of ancient goddess cults on one hand, and on the other to the type of fairy tale in which the hero must defeat a giant to possess the princess. Each of these traditions is informed by the oedipal theme; the incidents of the fourteenth-

century English poem *Sir Gawain and the Green Knight* illustrate this theme
and demonstrate the relationship of the courtly love myth to the year's king
ritual and giant-killer fairy tale traditions.

In this poem, Sir Gawain as the questing hero goes in search of the "giant"
he must attempt to defeat, the boastful Green Knight who has already shown
himself indestructible by ordinary means. Gawain's first encounter with the
Green Knight has ended indecisively; although he defeated the antagonist at
Arthur's court by beheading him, the Green Knight magically survives, and
now Gawain must submit to him in a second encounter. Thus far, we have the
incident preserved from what is apparently the tale's source, the symbolic
death and resurrection of the Holly King, discussed by Robert Graves in *The
White Goddess*. Also, we see a situation familiar in folk and fairy tales, the
hero's frustration in his at-first apparently successful attempt to overcome
obstacles in his path.

Next, Gawain, on his way to find the Green Knight, becomes the guest of
the Lord of the Forest Castle. Here, in the central incident of the tale, we see
the incest theme almost explicitly revealed. Gawain's host is doubly a father-
figure, for he is not only the strange Lord but also the disguised Green Knight.
He goes out hunting every day for three days, bringing Gawain the game he
has killed, and exchanging the game (a figure for the father's sustenance of the
child) for kisses (a figure for the child's gratitude, filial affection). The kisses
that Gawain bestows upon his host have been acquired from the Lady of the
castle, the host's wife. Gawain has met this woman in the company of a
second, older, "matronly" female, who is later revealed to have been Morgan
Le Faye, Gawain's aunt, Arthur's half-sister, whose magic was responsible for
the Green Knight's supernatural powers, and whose relationship to Gawain,
Arthur, and Arthur's illegitimate son by her own sister makes her appearance
here a reminder of the incest theme.

The Lady comes to Gawain fully clothed while he lies in bed, and though
he is tempted to commit adultery he contents himself with kisses. On the third
occurrence of the Lady's visit, however, he accepts the gift of her girdle, which
he keeps a secret from the Lord. Finally, after he has met the Green Knight
and taken the blow he had agreed to receive, Gawain finds that his host and
the Knight are the same, that the two feigned blows struck by the Knight were
in return for the kisses, and that the third blow, wounding Gawain slightly,
was in repayment for the girdle, which Gawain must now wear as a symbol of
his dishonesty (in not revealing that gift to his host) and of his cowardice (in
shrinking from the first two blows).

What is significant here is that the host had instructed his wife to act as
she had, testing Gawain, but after the mystery has been cleared up between the
two men the blame is pointedly given to the woman; in fact, the woes suffered
by men because of women are recounted in a long series of Old Testament

examples. Also, the sin of adultery (veiling the more troubling one of incest) is not attributed to Gawain, although by accepting the Lady's girdle he has symbolically cuckolded her husband. Rather, he is said to be guilty of dishonesty, because he kept the gift a secret, and especially of cowardice, again for having kept the gift a secret but also for flinching from the "punishment" delivered by his host.

Such tales as this one fulfilled a number of cultural and psychological needs at the time of their currency. In the Gawain story, the desired adultery/incest is both avoided through the virtue and strength of the hero (he is tempted but does not submit to the temptation) and fulfilled symbolically through his acceptance of the Lady's girdle. The antagonism toward the father is acted out in the beheading of the Green Knight and in the defiance Gawain flings at him after their second encounter; but the relationship is repaired through the Green Knight's wounding of Gawain and their mutual assignment of blame to the Lady, and also through Gawain's fealty to Arthur expressed in his acceptance of the Green Knight's challenge.

One of the greatest values of this tale, and of the literature of courtly love in general, is its quality of distance from the ordinary life of the audience. Not only are the characters elevated by nobility, but they are said to have existed in ancient times. The magical events serve not only to explain otherwise incomprehensible elements of symbolism but also to remove the tale even further from human experience. In *The Uses of Enchantment,* Bruno Bettelheim argues that remote settings and unlikely or magical events provide psychological distancing that allows a reader to escape too close identification with fictional characters. While Bettelheim stresses the value of such distance in fairy tales for children, it seems likely that such devices serve the same purpose in adult mythic literature. In the sentimental/Gothic myth, the lack of distance distorts the way in which mythic material is expressed and interpreted. The figure of the father or giant must be presented as a real man of authority, and the son's hostility toward him must be sublimated because it cannot be outwardly expressed. The "knight" himself, unaided by either magic or doctrine, must rely on the Lady's virtue to curb his unconsciously incestuous passion; thus all passion becomes threatening and sinful. And the Lady's physical frailty is both an attempt to avoid sexuality (by denying desire on her part) and a covert punishment for unacknowledged but nevertheless projected sexual guilt.

The female figure of the sentimental myth presents still another problem. To portray a woman as both dangerously passionate and attractive, when she is supposed to represent real female nature but in fact carries the incestuously attractive component of the mythic female figure as well, is too disturbing to be attempted in the sentimental tradition. However, the portrayal of a "real" woman as angelic, superhumanly virtuous, was not beyond the scope of the light side of the myth, whose makers were compelled to disguise or destroy any conscious reminders of the incest theme. The terror and passion, which in courtly love literature are invoked simultaneously by female figures sufficiently distanced from the reader, find their expression within the overt contradictions and the Gothic side of the later myth.

The mother-son incest commonly expressed figuratively by adultery in courtly love literature is sometimes found in Gothic literature as well, although in most instances the relationship is characterized by hostility (as in *The Monk,* with Ambrosio's murder of the woman who will turn out to have been his mother, or in *Dracula* with the death of Lucy's mother from fear of Dracula in the shape of a wolf), but more often the incestuous relationship is between brother and sister or brother-sister substitutes *or* between father and daughter or father-daughter substitutes. Further, in the literature of courtly love the relationship between the two characters was seldom represented as overtly incestuous, but it was often portrayed as overtly sexual, even if physical consummation was not accomplished or was accomplished symbolically, as in the Gawain tale. Violence between the protagonist and his beloved was relatively infrequent, although the protagonist's unrequited or unwillingly aroused passion—as in the Gawain episode—might cause harm or pain to *him.* The violence was, instead, between the protagonist and the father-figure, who was sometimes the woman's actual father, her protector or captor, but more often her husband. The desired incest was often masked by the portrayed crime of adultery.

In Gothic literature, incest is quite often portrayed overtly—sometimes the characters are aware of the nature of their relationship, and sometimes the consanguinity is discovered after sexual consummation has occurred. But when the relationship is overtly or covertly incestuous—or even when it is not overtly sexual—it is generally colored by violence, committed by the protagonist or other agents or forces upon the person of the woman. Adultery is relatively rare in Gothic literature; incest is characteristically masked, if it is masked at all, by the violent crimes of assault, murder, or other violation (such as vampirism). Finally, while the doubling that allowed simultaneous hostility and respect toward the father-figure of courtly love literature—if the ambivalence was not in fact allowed to appear without division or doubling—occurred not within the character of the protagonist but in figures representing the father (as Arthur, the Green Knight, and the Lord of the Forest Castle in the Gawain tale represent this figure), the characteristic doubling that occurs in the Gothic is of the protagonist, the reader's surrogate, who is himself split into various characters or doppelgängers.

These differences between courtly love and Gothic literature suggest that the incestuous relationships common to the Gothic must be interpreted as having a different significance than solely the portrayal of oedipal emotions (although such emotions, necessarily associated, are no doubt responsible for much of the disguising of events, characters, and responses that takes place). Were the idea of incest so threatening that it alone necessitated the exaggerated atmosphere of terror or the disintegration of the protagonist's personality, both indispensible characteristics of the Gothic, it seems unlikely that the undisguised act of incest would be overtly portrayed so often as the Gothic portrays it. In fact, incest—brother-sister incest especially but also the incestuous relationship involving father and daughter—is itself symbolic in Gothic literature of another sort of union: the reconciliation of the feminine and masculine within the personality of a single individual.

The reconciliation of these supposedly mutually exclusive qualities within the same individual is, as we have seen, abhorrent to the sentimental/Gothic myth in one sense; the clear definition and separation of masculinity and femininity as mythic qualities depends, in the supposedly realistic sentimental tradition, upon their strict separateness as sexual identities and sex roles. Still, even in the sentimental side of the myth one can see that their reconciliation is actively sought; this is apparent in the myth's insistence upon the sentimental love relationship, in which the two principals are supposed to be spiritually attracted to each other, soul mates, two halves of a better whole, members of a union that the romantic poets were quick to characterize figuratively (and in many cases without Gothic terror) as the relationship, often incestuous, of brother and sister. Further, this figuratively employed relationship, symbolic of a spiritual reuniting of the disparate parts of the self, often takes the form of a father-daughter relationship in reflection of the nature of masculine and feminine roles: the active and powerful masculine figure, identifiable as a strong, fatherly character, always stands more or less in the relationship of father to the passive, powerless woman who represents ideal femininity. The masculine role of protector and supporter, together with the feminine role of sexually unawakened (or asexual) woman-child, both mythic representations, suggest the unequal father-daughter relationship; this suggestion is strengthened by the actual disparity in ages that often results from adherence to the sentimental courtship code.

Violence, which is almost always part of the Gothic portrayal of such relationships, results from the contradictory sentimental expectation that a reconciliation between masculinity and femininity be sought and at the same time avoided, that the masculine man and feminine woman retain within themselves the integrity of their roles while achieving a union that transcends their roles' integrity. Such conflicting ideals, reflected in the pursuit-and-flight game of courtship, are carried to their logical concluson in the Gothic, which portrays both men and women deliberately pursuing the forbidden relationship at the same time that they both deliberately attempt to avoid it by the expedient of destroying the weaker, passive feminine figure. The fact that pursuit or avoidance is often accidental, or that one participant is active while the other is apparently passive in this pursuit and flight, does not alter the deliberateness of both conflicting actions—attempted reconciliation and attempted avoidance of reconciliation—by both participants, either of whom may be represented by doppelgängers. Symbolically, the passive or feminine attitude is in fact as positive a figure of the conflicting desires for separation and union as is the active or masculine role.

Incest, says Masao Miyoshi in *The Divided Self,* was for the romantics a figure for self-division and the discovery of the self's identity (11). The theme of incest, says Thomas Thornburg, "marks Dracula's relations with his conquests, who are his daughters, his sisters, and his mistresses all in one. The whole world of vampirism is one of convoluted incestuous relationships" (33). In the Gothic, a sort of cultural nightmare in which boundaries of identity fixed in the normal world have little meaning, each character and object is in some degree a part of the protagonist, as the people and objects in dreams are part of the dreamer. Every sexual or symbolically sexual relationship is in some way a proposed union with the self. And while the urgency with which such a union—or reunion—is desired is reflected in the preoccupation of the Gothic with sexual relationships and symbols, including the forbidden relationship of incest, the union is feared and resented with equal intensity.

Everything that the sentimental tradition designates as masculine or feminine—including the demonically violent excess of one and the death-seeking excess of the other—would be taken, were such a union permitted, into each individual, who is afforded no distant or dogmatic archetypal projections of those forces as protection from their interference in his or her conscious life. Thus the union of the self is violently opposed even as it is sought. The fictional character representing total femininity is pursued, suffers prolonged agonies, and then dies. If her fictional death is sometimes averted at the last moment, this too is a form of masking; the gratification at her impending death has already been experienced. She desires union with the masculine character and she desires her own death; the character representing the masculine ideal or potential ideal desires to be united with her and desires her death; he wishes to be deprived of his excessive masculinity and wishes to retain it. Thus the apparently contradictory motives of such characters as Clarissa and Lovelace are explained. The Gothic is a dramatization of conflicting desires, and its movement is complex: toward unity with the sister-lover anima, and toward her destruction; toward the defeat of the violent, demonic forces that prey on her (the forces that, separated and despised by the sentimental world view, threaten the destruction of that world view), and toward the terrible triumph of those forces.

The fragmentation of characters implied in the Gothic complexity of motive begins in the sentimental side of the myth, with behavioral ambiguity that suggests deeply conflicting motives within characters who are otherwise presented as more or less singly, if not simplistically, motivated. Often a character's actions (for example, Rochester's apparent cruelty when he seems to court Blanche Ingram and forces Jane to watch, in *Jane Eyre,* or Beth's insistence on nursing the sick child and exposing herself and her family to the illness they know is contagious, in *Little Women*) seem perversely at odds with what we must believe about that character to accept him or her as a good person; often, too, such actions are never explained satisfactorily—Rochester later says he wished to make Jane jealous in order to win her love, for example, yet he has had no reason to suppose that as long as his wife is unknown to her she could not be won in a fairer way. Thus the apparent depth of a character implied by the ambiguous behavior seems to be unintentional, at least on a conscious level, for that facet of the personality is simply never revealed again, nor does it figure again in the plot or in the other characters' perceptions or actions. We must believe Rochester's explanation of his cruelty, and we must believe Jane's acceptance of his explanation, although neither is quite believable; we must accept that Beth has in this instance resisted her sisters' influence and behaved with an independence she never exhibits in any other instance. Yet the unconscious motive, revealing Gothic complexities within sentimental characters, can never be completely dismissed from the reader's conscious or unconscious awareness.

For example, let us consider the characterizations in *Clarissa,* a deeply sentimental novel with undeniably Gothic overtones. The ambiguity of both central characters' motives provides much of this immensely popular novel's intensity of dramatic interest, yet the novel offers little if any rational explanation for this ambiguity, nor do the characters themselves seem aware of it. Clarissa's attraction to Lovelace is responsible not only for her elopement with him, but also for her continued hope that he will reform and behave toward her as a lover ought—that his love for her will domesticate him. Despite the increasingly unavoidable signs that this will never happen, Clarissa remains attracted to him, as she admits in letter after letter to Anna Howe, and if her attraction is based partly on her hopes for his reform as she insists, we still feel it must be based as well on her awareness of her probable defeat. Lovelace's ambiguity is just as obvious, and because it is more actively expressed it strikes us even more than Clarissa's as a sign of conflicting motive unacknowledged by the character. Even as his actions and fantasies express an unmistakable desire for dominance that amounts to destruction, Lovelace continues to refer to Clarissa, in his letters, in terms of endearment, and we can have no doubt that he means these loving remarks sincerely. In *Richardson's Characters,* Morris Golden notes the instances of sadistic fantasy, involving not only Clarissa but also Anna Howe, Anna's mother, and various other women, in Lovelace's correspondence; Golden argues a comparison with

Samuel Richardson's own fantasies, as revealed in his own correspondence, that suggests either a surprising degree of self-knowledge and self-revelation on Richardson's part or a depth of psychological characterization of which the author himself was not entirely aware.

Conflicting motives within a character are expressed not only by ambiguous behavior but also, even within sentimental literature, by doubling, the reinforcement or substitution of characters by or for each other. In addition to the signs of dividedness within both central characters in *Clarissa,* we find secondary characters who, while they are necessary for the plot and the epistolary device, function *as characters* mainly as extensions of, or alternatives to, the roles of Lovelace and Clarissa. James Harlowe, Clarissa's brother, is a type of Lovelace; Golden points out that Lovelace's passion to dominate is, in the first part of the novel, pitted against that of "the cruder James" (14), but there is really no conflict between these two except for the material possession of Clarissa. They are much alike in motive and manner, and Lovelace "wins" the battle between them as much by virtue of the fact that Richardson's plot demands his winning as by his more subtle, certainly more intelligent, pursuit of his object. Anna Howe, besides functioning as Clarissa's correspondent, is also a foil against whom Clarissa's character may be shown. But Anna reveals Clarissa by being like, rather than unlike, her friend. She is in a position to be more realistic, more cynical, to give advice. But she is probably no more intelligent than Clarissa nor less susceptible, physically or psychologically, to masculine power; she is only considerably luckier in her family relationships. Indeed, Anna must not be morally superior to Clarissa; were she so, she would usurp interest and admiration that must be retained by the novel's heroine.

Clarissa's escape from the stupid and repellent man her brother has chosen for her is really an escape from James himself, and in regard to her freedom it is no escape at all. She is surrounded from the beginning by sadistic masculinity, with her brother and his protégé on one side and her lover on the other. These male characters all represent degrees of excessive masculinity threatening Clarissa's feminine helplessness, and if one appears monstrous while another seems to offer the protection and support expected by sentimental tradition, the balance soon shifts; when James and his proposed suitor disappear as threats (except inasmuch as they continue to prevent Clarissa's return to her family), the threat reappears in the form of Lovelace himself.

The female characters, too, represent a doubling so that femininity may be presented in various degrees and reinforced in various permutations of the feminine role. There is no reason to suppose that, had Anna been placed in the same position as Clarissa, she would have behaved differently. Thus, in addition to her function as Clarissa's correspondent and advisor, Anna serves as an extension of Clarissa's character, a double who shares the essential feminine powerlessness, who suffers emotionally along with Clarissa, and who bears the brunt as well of Lovelace's hostility and the violence of his fantasies.

Morris Golden finds that the chief difference between the two young women is in "upbringing," Clarissa being as a result of hers more dutiful and "refined" than her friend (50). However, Clarissa is scarcely a submissively feminine young lady at the beginning of the novel, nor is her elopement with Lovelace a dutiful or refined act; her antisentimental behavior here is, of course, necessary to the plot, but it is demanded as well by the sentimental insistence upon romantic love between the members of a courting couple. (This same insistence demands that Clarissa and Lovelace continue to perceive their relationship as a loving one, even during its most violent episodes, so that her earlier independence will not be repeated.) Anna's greater degree of independence, later in the novel, seems less a function of her own character than of her mother's; she has more opportunity, not fewer scruples, than her friend. In fact, we have no way of judging until Clarissa is called upon to show her remarkable tenacity of virtue that she *will* show it, and no way of knowing that Anna, in the same situation, would not.

Even Mrs. Sinclair, apparently the heroine's opposite in all respects, is a double for Clarissa in some respects, representing an aspect of womanhood, if not of femininity, that Clarissa must struggle to the death to avoid. Mrs. Sinclair is repellent because she has long ago discarded passive femininity and succumbed to the perverse masculine passions in her own character (so that she functions, incidentally, as a double for Lovelace as well). But she, like Clarissa, is subject to Lovelace's masculine dominance, and her hideous but fascinatingly drawn death is Clarissa's reflected in a Gothic mirror. Mrs. Sinclair's name, in fact, reveals her relationship to the heroine: almost an anagram for *Clarissa, Sinclair* also spells out what Clarissa, flawed or sinful, might become.

If division and duplication of character exist within the sentimental side of the divided myth, these phenomena are much more apparent in the Gothic. The concept of the doppelgänger or double is one that pervades Gothic literature; it is, in fact, to be found throughout the literature and art of the nineteenth century, as Miyoshi demonstrates, and as the ease with which we may recall examples—Hoffmann's "The Doppelgänger," Poe's "William Wilson," Stephenson's *Dr. Jekyll and Mr. Hyde,* Wilde's *Picture of Dorian Gray,* Rosetti's painting "How They Met Themselves"—reminds us. The significance of the concept as both a literary and a psychological phenomenon has been explored by a number of writers (two interesting studies are Ralph Tymms's *Doubles in Literary Psychology* and Robert Rogers's *A Psychoanalytic Study of the Double in Literature*), who in general may be said to agree upon several points. The concept apparently reflects a psychologically real event that may be experienced as dream or hallucination, and often arises from some sort of division of consciousness or motive. It has often been recognized as a supernatural or preternatural occurrence, and may be encountered in various forms throughout the literature and myth of various cultures.

A distinction is sometimes made between two types or modes of doppelgänger, the double by duplication and the double by division. Tymms discusses this distinction especially in reference to folk tales and myths in which the double appears. Both modes of doubling seem to operate in the literary use of this concept; for example, Jekyll and Hyde would appear to be doubles by division, having both originated in the undivided character of Jekyll, whereas Poe's narrator and Wilson are apparently doubles by duplication, having encountered each other for the first time at school and having been born—if the story is to be taken realistically in any sense—to two different sets of parents. However, the concept seems in general to represent division, at least as it functions symbolically in Gothic literature, as is usually shown by the conflicting actions, motives, or natures exhibited by the set of doubles, implying conflicts in the original character that can be expressed only by a division of that character into two or more personae. The double by duplication, often seen in mythic literature as an instance of a supernatural, often malign, spirit disguising itself by assuming the features of a living person, seems to represent an attempt to explain psychological division within an individual as perceived by others or even by that individual. Instances of doubling by duplication do occur in literature when the pair or set of characters is necessary not for the expression of conflicting motives but for reinforcement of the concept represented by one character; the set of protagonists in *Dracula,* a group of young men essentially indistinguishable from one another in personal characteristics, is an instance of duplication for reinforcement, necessary to support the depleted masculinity of the hero in the presence of the overwhelmingly excessive masculinity of the antagonist.

However this doppelgänger or second self is perceived as originating, and whatever its behavior (often, especially when the concept is not elaborated as a literary device—that is, when it appears to be an actual occurrence—the double is merely glimpsed or otherwise momentarily sensed), it is a disturbing experience, and the sense of uncanniness and horror it engenders makes it a natural choice for inclusion in the Gothic cabinet of weird paraphernalia. But, like the vampire and the Gothic ruin itself, the doppelgänger has a significance for the myth beyond its effectiveness as a contributor to the atmosphere of terror.

The figure of the double seems to have been suggested to some artists and writers by personal experience. Stephenson and Rosetti both reported dreams in which doppelgängers figured, and the individuals cited these dreams as sources of artistic inspiration. Likewise, if Victor Frankenstein and the Monster are doubles, then Mary Shelley's dream from which her novel grew was a similar instance. Shelley himself, especially given to hallucination by most accounts, had dreams and waking visions in which figures of his friends and of himself appeared as the individuals' doubles. Jane Williams, apparently one of the least fanciful members of the Shelley circle, saw Shelley's double a few weeks before his death. None of this is surprising when one reflects that dreams, like other imaginative experiences, were welcomed and taken seriously by artists of the period; that every figure in a dream is, in a sense, a double of the dreamer; and above all that the idea of the double, once introduced into the artistic consciousness of the time, was bound to reinforce itself, to become more available as it became more familiar. The dividedness that has been argued as characteristic of the period made the double, a concept used in literature since ancient times, an especially appropriate metaphor for this time.

A well-known example of the metaphor's use is the appearance, in Shelley's *Prometheus Unbound,* of phantasms and spirits that are explained to Prometheus by The Earth as "The shadows of all forms that think and live...Dreams and the light imaginings of men" (I, lines 198, 200). The double, as Shelley describes it here, may be either "terrible" or "sublime"; it may be the shade of a living person or supernatural being, or it may be an imagined or idealized form. Shelley's conception of the double is surely related to his own dividedness, his pursuit, as Christopher Small in *Ariel Like a Harpy* argues it, of the Ariel ideal, while he is in turn pursued by his Caliban shadow. It is especially notable, in view of Victor Frankenstein's characterization of the Monster as "my own vampire, my own spirit let loose from the grave" (77), that all the doubles described in *Prometheus Unbound,* whether terrible or sublime, exist "underneath the grave" in the world of death. The double, as a sign or symptom of dividedness, need not be monstrous; but, given the nature of the sentimental/Gothic dichotomy, in which the rejected concepts and truths of experience are thrust out of sight into the world of death and the demonic, the monstrous double of the Gothic is inevitable.

Let us consider instances of doubling in Stoker's *Dracula,* a reflection of the sentimental/Gothic conflict so divided and fractured that its doubles are in fact tripled and quadrupled, polarized fragments of beings desperately reinforcing one another as they struggle against the great evil whose essential unrecognized kinship with them invests the novel with much of its horror and fascination.

Although vampirism, not the double, is *Dracula*'s central figure, the book is permeated with division and duplication, reflecting conflicts not only within characters but also in point of view, plot, and setting. The story is told through a collection of documents—journals, letters, even recordings—whose "authors," the book's five major narrators, speak or write in distinctly different voices. Their efforts to collate the various documents, and the difficulties they encounter in these efforts, account for many of the plot complications. The plot itself is deeply divided, so that for nearly half the book's length there is no apparent connection between Jonathan Harker's adventures on his journey to Dracula's stronghold, the mysterious illness of his fiancée's friend Lucy, and the strange case of Renfield, who is a patient at the lunatic asylum run by one of Lucy's rejected suitors. The plot achieves a degree of unity when Van Helsing, an acquaintance of the doctor's, suspects a connection among the various events and attempts to synthesize the information collected by the characters; this unifying influence is pure coincidence, for Van Helsing's suspicion is based on an unlikely interest in vampire lore. The setting itself remains divided, with the novel beginning and ending in the wild Carpathian Mountains and reaching its turning point in England.

Dracula's characters are so complexly divided that *doubling* scarcely describes their fragmentation. The protagonist is really a *set* of characters; Johnathan Harker and Lucy's three suitors—John Seward, Quincy Morris, and Arthur Godalming—are scarcely distinct from one another in a duplication necessary to balance the terrible power of the antagonist; and the fatherly Van Helsing is needed to reinforce further this depleted army of sentimental masculinity. Even Renfield, at first apparently on the antagonist's side, is part of the protagonist set, for while his madness (like Harker's naïveté) has helped to give Dracula access to England, his final struggle is against the vampire. Even the numbers of the protagonist set do not guarantee their victory; not only are Renfield and Quincy Morris killed before the battle is over, but the final defeat of Dracula is so ambiguously worded that the reader is left in some doubt as to its real finality.

Femininity is portrayed in *Dracula* by two major characters, Lucy and Jonathan's fiancée Mina, at first apparently the familiar fair and dark ladies who cannot, in the sentimental tradition, actually represent two extremes of good and evil. Mina is the fair or good woman, treated by the members of the protagonist set as a cross between goddess and mother, untouched by sexuality—even after her marriage, as has been noted, because of Jonathan's depletion of masculinity after his encounter with Dracula—and the threatened victim whose fragility and purity the protagonists struggle to protect. (It should be noted that Mina's taming of Jonathan, and by extension of the other male characters, parallels Dracula's invasion of their lives; their depletion of masculinity is actually the Gothic revelation of the true nature of what is, from the sentimental point of view, their ideally masculine state. In symbolic terms, *Dracula* depicts the "creation" of the "monster" as a necessary part of the rejection of excessive masculinity, masked by a reversal of causality.)

Lucy seems at first to be no less feminine than Mina, and indeed she approaches ideal femininity as she nears her first, false, death (in the moments when she is *not* under the sensualizing influence of Dracula), and realizes it at the moment of her "true" death, when her fiancé and the other men recognize and comment upon the loveliness of her features. But Lucy's perverse masculinity, barely hinted in the sensuality that allows her to welcome three suitors without being able to decide immediately which she will marry, is further revealed in her sensuous reaction to Dracula's vampiric rape and finally made plain in her monstrous transformation into the "bloofer lady" who, as Dracula's minion, feeds on innocent living children.

Dracula himself, the dark and monstrous doppelgänger representing excessive masculinity, is so powerful that every other antagonistic force in the novel draws its strength directly from him, could be nothing without him—is, in a sense, part of him. Moreover, he is the real unifying element of the novel, the common denominator of all the documents, moving steadily at the center of the fragmented plot, determining the setting by his orders and movements, drawing the characters together before they are even aware of one another's existence. Dracula is a tremendous figure to embody the Gothic elements separated and suppressed by the myth; his age, noble birth, and loyalty to a glorious feudal past are reminders of a culture and time that the sentimental world at once rejects and yearns for. He is both intensely attractive and intensely repellent; in no other Gothic figure are eroticism and death so completely integrated and so uncompromisingly linked. And even in his excessive masculinity, beyond sentimental hope of taming, Dracula reveals the sentimental masculine/feminine dichotomy as arbitrary. Even Mina's pure femininity is imperiled when, through the blundering of the protagonists, she herself is attacked by the vampire. Now imbued with his masculine strength and passion, she exhibits signs of sensuality that horrify her and the men, and her impurity is signaled by the scarlet mark imprinted on her forehead when Van Helsing touches her with a consecrated Host. Mina's most believable emotion in the novel is her reaction to this development, an ambiguous combination of disgust, shame, anxiety, and voluptuousness—in other words, a typical response of a person forced to an unwilling awareness of his or her sexuality, an awareness too dangerous for the sentimental convention to accept. What Lucy has been, Mina may become. Thus Lucy and Mina, each other's doubles, further doubled in their own vampire selves (though Mina never quite achieves this state) and redoubled in the sisters at

Dracula's castle, are finally revealed as female doubles of Dracula himself, related to him by the sentimentally unacceptable traits that, rejected and suppressed, turn monstrous.

Femininity and masculinity, both fragmented in *Dracula,* are thus shown to be indistinct from each other. The depleted masculinity of the men, like the perversely imbued masculinity of the women, is accomplished by the towering figure of Dracula, who is the distorted mirror image of them all. Dracula is the projected and rejected doppelgänger who threatens order, reason, morality, human consciousness, and conscience and offers timeless vitality in return— the Gothic completion that shows sentimentality its own instability and incompleteness. He does not threaten the individual existence of his victims, but instead threatens the civilized structure they require to retain their sentimentally defined human identities.

What they demand of him, consciously, is his annihilation. His deathlessness is a threat and an insult to their mortality. But his deathlessness—Van Helsing uses the term *Undead* to refer to the vampire—is not life, for it is in itself incomplete and sterile. Dracula's death must take place, and the mortality of the protagonist set and their lady be assured, for their human existence to continue; Dracula's *true* death is, symbolically, the true integration of his vitality with their civility. The irony is that without Dracula their world is as incomplete and sterile as his. Because he is their double, they must somehow partake of him or they themselves will be shadows. Thus, the otherwise inexplicable method of Lucy's "true" death, insisted upon by Van Helsing, with all the members of the protagonist set except Renfield violating her body with sharpened stakes, and the similar final attack on Dracula (with a knife substituted for the stake), are necessary for the men whom he has depleted of masculine force to regain that force, penetrating and symbolically feminizing the excessively masculine monster. And thus Dracula's death is necessary for Mina to attain womanhood, accepting the rejected characteristics—sensuality and power—forbidden to femininity, and for her marriage to Jonathan to become fruitful.

The child born to Mina on "the same day as that on which Quincey Morris died" (382)—that is, the day on which Dracula was defeated, although the phrase is obviously intended to mean the anniversary of that day—is given the names of all the members of the protagonist set; symbolically, the child is fathered by all of them just as they were all united to Lucy by transfusions of blood and by the act of her death. But as their union with Lucy was in turn a union with Dracula, whose blood had been mingled with hers. so is their relationship with Mina and her child necessarily a union with him. Their return to Dracula's castle with the child, a year after its birth, can be for no other purpose than the celebration of the baby's other father, the part of its human nature they must always reject but can never escape or truly destroy.

Dracula's vampire nature shows very clearly, in several respects, the relationship between the monstrous Gothic doppelgänger and its supposedly normal partner, as this relationship had developed by the late nineteenth century. Once human, the vampire is now only superficially so. He is, in every respect, evil and unholy. He is totally opposed to human enterprise and civilization as they are defined in the conscious sentimental tradition. While the normal human being is weak, restricted, mortal, the vampire is powerful, protean, deathless. While the urge of human civilization, sentimentally defined, is to destroy all traces of the vampire, the vampire's urge is to make all like him, a part of him. He is responsible for his own being, capable of great control of himself and of others, but in terms of sentimentally defined civilization—since it rejects him and thus rejects control of him as well—absolutely irresponsible for all else; as Van Helsing says, he is "childlike," and it is only in this sense (his irresponsibility, his lawless existence) that the epithet can be understood: the vampire takes no real heed of the future. On the other hand, the sentimentally defined human being on whom his sights are set is incapable of control, either of the vampire or of himself or herself, until the human being performs the ceremonial act by which the vampire is destroyed.

This act is, from the point of view of sentimentality, one of annihilation; from the Gothic point of view, it is an act of integration. Just as the creation of the monster and the *rejection* of the monster are in fact the same, so are the acceptance and the destruction of the monster identical. The vampire simply cannot be destroyed by ordinary means, nor can the Gothic be wiped out of existence by the sentimental. The ceremonial, symbolic act of destruction/ integration must be carried out by the sentimental individual, who has retained human will as a conscious characteristic, and must be resisted until the end by the vampire, whose childish *willfulness* is actually a stubborn, human vitality that refuses to yield to sentimental mastery. Yet the act is significantly erotic, the impalement on a stake—a mirror image of the impalement practiced by the vampire himself—and the vampire's final look of "peace," followed by his physical disappearance, suggests not so much destruction as union with the sentimental protagonist.

But although *Dracula* suggests a possible healing of the sentimental/ Gothic dichotomy, it also shows how divided the myth had become and how consequently threatening the Gothic appeared to the sentimental consciousness by the closing years of the nineteenth century. The vampire doppelgänger is voracious in his hunger and is nourished from the very being of his mortal counterpart. He is stronger, quicker, more cunning, and he uses his power to sap youth, will, resistance, finally existence—that is, existence as a mortal being conscious of his or her own identity—from the victim. As the other's strength fails, the vampire's is constantly increased. Only the fact that his reflection does not appear in the mirror that reflects the mortal being reveals that the vampire has no independent existence. He is separate, but is finally a part of the person who is actually reflected.

Within the sentimental/Gothic myth, the Gothic is a doppelgänger of the sentimental, as a whole and in all of its parts. It is at the same time a refutation and an extension of the sentimental, a completion of the myth. By the late nineteenth century, the Gothic doppelgänger had achieved a power so disproportionate that its original nature is only hinted in Stoker's novel. The significance of the Gothic lies most surely in its manner of emergence, its separation or creation, and in its relationship to its sentimental counterpart at the moment of its emergence. For in creating and rejecting it, the sentimental awareness determines the nature of the Gothic and of itself. To discern plainly the nature of the monster as creature, child, and alter ego of the troubled hero of sentimental myth, we must turn to the first third of the nineteenth century and to Mary Shelley's *Frankenstein.*

2

Frankenstein and the Monster

Antisentimental Irony: Victor and Walton

Because one side of the sentimental/Gothic myth is consciously suppressed and masked in Gothic figures, the unsuppressed, conscious side has frequently been seen as an irrational pattern of thought and behavior, a personal and social code whose adoption, for whatever reason or reasons, is at least foolish and, at worst, potentially damaging to the individual and society. Thus, writers and social critics have produced antisentimental expressions, ranging in tone from serious cultural criticism—for example, Mary Wollstonecraft's feminist writings—to relatively gentle satire and irony by such writers as William Thackeray and Jane Austen. Such writers were themselves, in most cases, greatly influenced by sentimental assumptions, which accounts for the fact that most antisentimental expressions are self-contradictory to some extent, accepting some parts of the sentimental code and inveighing against others. Dickens, for example, can criticize the sentimental tradition's damaging conception of women, satirize the sort of woman who seems willingly to participate in and encourage this conception, and still reveal his own deeply imbued belief in the code he criticizes—all of this, often, within the same novel.

Mary Shelley's *Frankenstein* is in one sense an antisentimental novel; that is, it is a novel in which the sentimental tradition is consciously invoked so that its flaws may be ironically revealed. The values espoused by characters in *Frankenstein* are those imposed by the sentimental tradition, the characters themselves are drawn according to that convention, and the settings and situations are in great part typical of the sentimental novel. Yet by manipulating point of view throughout the book, Mary Shelley undermines the values, characters, and situations, ironically revealing the sentimental tradition's basically flawed, irrational, incomplete, and untenable nature.

Unlike other antisentimental works, such as *Jane Eyre,* in which the irony is achieved by setting an unsentimental character against the sentimental conventions (and thus undermining those conventions more or less openly),

Frankenstein is covertly antisentimental; the characters with whom the reader is invited to sympathize are themselves determinedly sentimental from start to finish. Victor Frankenstein, who is both instrument and victim of the book's irony, is aware of the irony only imperfectly. The only character who actually comes to a perception of the sentimental tradition's flawed nature is the Monster, the novel's apparent antagonist, with whom the reader is not free to sympathize openly. Thus *Frankenstein*'s antisentimental nature is withheld, bound up with the book's Gothic, mirror-image truths in a way that arouses and maintains the reader's anxiety and never quite dispels it. *Frankenstein* remains, overtly, a novel of sentiment in which the Gothic Monster is the antagonist; it is not apparently antisentimental, for the irony that would make it so cannot be recognized directly. The points of view that would need to be reconciled for complete recognition to occur remain disparate, always drawn to one another but always drifting apart.

Point of view is very carefully controlled. The "main" part of the story, presented and framed by the Walton letters, is Victor's narrative. Everything within this narrative, including the descriptions of every character but Walton and Frankenstein, the events of the plot and the order in which they are related, the descriptions of setting, and even the central narrative of the Monster, is given us in Victor's words, determined by his sentimental judgment and understanding, prefaced by his stated purpose of instructing Walton so that the explorer may "deduce an apt moral from [the] tale" (30). Frankenstein's intention that his tale may be used as a moral guide, a conventionally sentimental apology for its telling, is all that dissuades him from letting the events of his story die with him—as they surely would, for their factual truth within the novel's context is ambiguous: they are either unprovable, because of the death of every possible witness besides Frankenstein and the Monster, or they are totally subjective events of Frankenstein's psyche, expressed in terms of an outward reality that exists for him alone. Though Frankenstein insists that his story will be proven true by "internal evidence" (30), he himself sees it as a moral allegory, a sort of romance arranged by fate or whatever force Victor believes to have been in control of its "series," by which his audience, Walton, may be "directed" or "consoled" in the success or failure of his own enterprise.

Victor's decision to tell his story is prompted by the coincidence of his finding so apt an audience as Walton and so appropriate a setting in which to tell it as the dreamlike polar icescape in which Walton's ship is locked. Like Walton, Victor recognizes the similarity and sympathy that make the two of them "brothers," and he knows that his story is so fantastic that it would scarcely be believed except in those "wild and mysterious regions" (30). He knows, too, having heard Walton's dreams of discovery, that the explorer is the very person who might understand his story and profit by it. But Victor's story, though told in the first person, is not given directly to the reader in the process of its being told to Walton; the story and Victor's rhetorical purpose in telling it are both related in Walton's own first-person narrative, the series of letters addressed to his sister, Margaret Seville (whose initials, as Veeder points out, are the same as Mary Shelley's).

We must recognize the importance of Walton as the direct narrator from whose point of view all three narratives are finally told. Walton, like Victor, is a person whom the sentimental tradition has shaped to such an extent that he is attempting to follow its conflicting dictates into what will obviously be disaster. His search for the highest pinnacle of rational knowledge, for whose sake he must "inure [his] body to hardship" (17) and in whose cause he must employ all of his "determined heart and resolved will" (23), is matched by his conviction that only the friendship of someone "gentle yet courageous, possessed of a cultivated as well as of a capacious mind" (19) can make such discovery worth while. Yet to achieve the first he must forego the second, for according to the sentimental tradition to which he is bound, such qualities as he requires can be conferred only by "gentle and feminine fosterage" (20), and are unlikely to be found in any who would share his ungentle, unfeminine quest.

As a sentimental protagonist, Walton is the ideal hero: his masculine qualities of reason, honor, courage, and passion are (at least in his own consciousness of them, communicated through his own point of view) perfectly balanced; and while they have not yet been tamed by the influence of the civilizing feminine qualities, the reader is aware that Walton is open to, even desirous of, such influence. Motherless, he has reached adulthood in an untamed, Byronic state, highly affected by the masculine company of his uncle, whose library of adventure stories was his early reading, the romantic poets whose works formed his later education, and the sailors with whom he has prepared himself for his voyage of exploration. But his letters to his sister (significantly named Seville—in British pronunciation nearly the word "civil") show by their content as well as by their frequency that he is amenable to her guidance, even as he travels further and further from any means by which it may be given to him.

Unlike Victor, Walton has not traveled so far, or become so divided, that he cannot be redeemed, but his steps in this direction make him the perfect sentimental male both to present the need for such redemption and to amplify the sentimenal values and code expressed in Frankenstein's tale. At the same time, his connection with Mrs. Seville, the possibility that he can turn back toward her, allows him to tell Frankenstein's story in a voice that is essentially sane, as Frankenstein's is not. It allows him to hear both Frankenstein and the

Monster, and to report the narrative of the one and the final despairing outcry of the other to the reader in the balanced fashion demanded of this novel's point-of-view character.

Victor Frankenstein, like the narrators of some of Poe's stories, is scarcely to be trusted as an objective reporter, and without some larger frame of reference his tale and in fact his very existence would be acceptable only conditionally, as romance and fantasy must always be conditionally accepted. Walton is the real person, the Wedding Guest, from whom we are able to accept Frankenstein, his story, and the Monster as being even ambiguously true. Without Walton's description of Frankenstein we would have no objective idea of this central character's probable state of mind; without Walton's reporting of the final appearance of the Monster we would have no real reason to believe in that character's objective existence.

Furthermore, the Walton letters with which the novel begins establish the sentimentality that it will go on to undermine. Walton's conventional middle-class English background, unusual only in that some unspecified accident has caused him to be brought up by an uncle and sister rather than by his natural parents, is apparent in what he tells us of his life. He has been too poor to have the advantages of a conventional genteel education, but he is definitely of a class that removes him from close fellowship with his English lieutenant, a person "unsoftened by cultivation" (20), and his ship's master, whose "wholly uneducated" state "detracts from the interest and sympathy" Walton would wish to give the friend he longs for (21).

Walton's sense of purpose, his conscious motive for the voyage he has undertaken, is entirely sentimental (as is Frankenstein's): he is desirous of personal adventure and glory, but at the same time he wishes to confer "inestimable benefit . . . on all mankind to the last generation" (16). The incongruity of these two motives is not apparent to Walton, but it is underscored for the reader by the vacillation between the two that Walton expresses in his letters, and especially by the contrast—its irony lost on Walton—between his comparing of his voyage to that of "a child . . . when he embarks in a little boat with his holiday mates" (16) and his arguing, immediately thereafter, of "inestimable benefit [to] mankind to the last generation," a phrase in itself ironic in view of the threat to human generation and generations he is about to encounter (and a phrase which unconsciously echoes the promise of the New Testament that Christ's blood will be on his persecutors' heads "until the last generation").

Similarly, Walton's undeniably sentimental attachment to his sister is emphasized not only by his repeated avowals of love and respect for her, but also by the fact that his letters are addressed to her at all; there is no indication, after all, that his uncle is not still living and more likely to be entertained and informed by the correspondence of a seafaring man. But the brotherly attachment and respect are undermined by an irony that, again, is not apparent to Walton. We have learned in the first sentence of the first letter that Mrs. Seville "regarded [the voyage] with such evil forebodings" (15). Still we find Walton reporting "one or two stiff gales, and the springing of a leak, . . . accidents which experienced navigators scarcely remember to record" (23)—but which cannot be supposed to reassure Margaret Seville, so why does this experienced navigator bother to report them?—and constantly referring to the possibility that he will never return, in a sort of Byronic pose that makes us as readers impatient with the man who has so emphatically professed his brotherly concern.

It is, however, Frankenstein's own narrative of his childhood and family life that establishes definitely the sentimental ideal in order that the ironies of that ideal may be exposed. What Frankenstein tells about his upbringing, a perfect enactment of sentimental roles and values, is often in conflict with what he inadvertently lets us know about that upbringing through some of the actions he relates. Also, his enthusiasm for the values that his family supposedly embodies is undermined by the ironically damaging effects of those values upon the lives of everyone concerned.

Kate Ellis has commented in detail on "the subversiveness of Shelley's critique of the family" that she finds in the history of Robert Walton's life and especially in "the more lengthily elaborated early life of Victor" (126, 127). Ellis notes the bourgeois background and assumptions of the Frankenstein family, the "forces that . . . separate domestic life from [masculine] work," the submissive feminine ideal, "the belief that material prosperity and social recognition are conferred on superior merit," and the essentially ineffectual and hypocritical attempts to remedy social ills with an extension of domestic affection, all of which sentimental values and beliefs are to be found in Victor's account of his early life (128, 130–31). What his narrative makes inescapably clear is the division between what the myth sees as masculinity and femininity.

It is the feminine ideal that Caroline Frankenstein exemplifies, as she labors to no avail to save her father's life, as she is cared for by her husband as "a fair exotic is sheltered by the gardener" (33), as she dies (in an actually pointless sacrifice of her life), "calmly . . . her countenance express[ing] affection even in death" (43). As Kate Ellis points out, the 1818 edition of *Frankenstein* has Caroline insisting upon caring for her adopted daughter, and so contracting her illness, *after* Elizabeth's recovery has been assured. In the 1831 version the daughter's life is still in jeopardy; Ellis wonders if the grim irony of the original version might not have seemed to Mary Shelley too obvious a comment on the self-destructive nature of the feminine ideal.

That ideal is even more strongly exemplified by Elizabeth, who is addressed as "cousin" by Victor (in the 1818 edition she is actually his aunt's child) but who is recalled as his "more than sister" (35). Elizabeth's "saintly soul . . . shone like a shrine-dedicated lamp in our peaceful home," says Victor; he continues: "She was the living spirit of love to soften and attract; I might have become sullen in my study, rough through the ardour of my nature, but that she was there to subdue me to semblance of her own gentleness" (38). And while she subdues Victor's passion, Elizabeth subdues the ambition of his friend Henry Clerval by "unfold[ing] to him the real loveliness of beneficence, and mak[ing] the doing good the end and aim of his soaring ambition" (38). Ironically, Elizabeth's influence on Victor's passionate will disappears immediately upon their first separation, at which point he pursues his own ends without apparent concern for their effect on her gentleness. Ironically, too, it is in Clerval's attempt to do good and to extend, at the expense of his own studies, the feminine influence for good upon Frankenstein that he loses his life, becoming the Monster's third victim.

As Ellis points out, the difference between masculine and feminine roles as Walton and Victor perceive them is essentially a difference between activity and passivity. The feminine principle is passive, weak, and in fact ineffectual, despite the role assigned to it of beneficent influence upon and control over the masculine principle. There are no bad or unfeminine women in the novel, as the female characters are presented from Victor's and Walton's points of view. All are drawn as gentle, exceedingly *soft* creatures, totally dependent upon men to give them knowledge of the world outside their domestic circles and to shelter them from its harsh realities. Caroline Frankenstein, who seems to the reader to have been independent in some degree—whose actions, in fact, are those of a strong, willful person—is said by Victor to have been left helpless, injured in health and spirit, upon the death of her father, whom she had supported. But despite his conviction of her helplessness, Victor reveals that Caroline was far more resilient than her own father and that she was apparently the real head of the household after her marriage: she adopted Elizabeth without even consulting her husband, and her deathbed wish that Victor and Elizabeth marry seems to have been responsible for Victor's father's insistence upon the marriage. Margaret Seville, though we are told very little of her, is by implication strong enough to have taken over responsibility for her brother's upbringing after their parents' deaths. Justine Moritz has left her original family (because of her mother's cruelty) and attached herself to Caroline Frankenstein, a remarkably independent act for a young woman of her time. Elizabeth herself, as we shall see, is largely responsible for manipulating Victor into marriage. All of these women are ironically revealed by their actions to be stronger and more willful than either Walton or Victor is capable of seeing.

Yet Caroline, Elizabeth, and Justine all suffer and die at least partly as a result of their own actions undertaken to fulfill the approved feminine role; they actually engage in their own destruction. Caroline contracts her fatal illness unnecessarily, for it is implied that other nurses for Elizabeth were available. Justine falls asleep and allows false evidence of murder to be left in her clothing; moreover, knowing that she is innocent of murder, she still fails to provide herself with a reasonable explanation of the evidence. Elizabeth marries Victor, who she has every reason to suspect is less than enthusiastic about their marriage (and whose mental unbalance she must certainly suspect), and waits obediently for him while the Monster forces his way into her bridal apartment. We know, from what Victor has told us of them, that all three of these women are capable of getting themselves through or out of difficult situations; yet when their lives are endangered they choose feminine, passive responses, resulting in each case in the woman's death.

Masculinity, here as in the sentimental novel generally, is seen as active, passionate, curious, ambitious, direct, forceful, effective. Walton, in defiance of his father's deathbed wishes, embarks on a course of exploration that takes him into dangerous territory far from his home. Victor Frankenstein's father, Alphonse, who has been an active, effective statesman, directs his family's actions (or so he apparently believes, and so Victor tells us) even in his retirement, travels to the British Isles to obtain his son's release from prison, urges the fatal marriage between Victor and Elizabeth. Victor himself, impelled by curiosity and a strangely compulsive ambition, pursues his mysterious studies to their successful conclusion. The Monster, as compulsively active as Victor, pursues his own destructive course with as much zeal and energy and with as definite effectiveness. Victor perceives Henry Clerval as strong, loyal, ambitious, honorable.

But Mary Shelley's irony in this novel undermines masculinity too. To both Victor and Walton, masculinity implies intellectual passion, the physical man trained to the spiritual purpose of knowing. Both are convinced that, in pursuing their goals, they are acting for the good of mankind and for their own fulfillment, and that they are somehow sacrificing their fondest *emotional* wishes, which they believe to be for the calm domestic pleasures of the essentially feminine circles they have left behind. Their ideal of masculinity is the Promethian ideal; it is, as Christopher Small has pointed out in *Ariel Like a Harpy,* the Shelleyan idea of unlimited imagination, "eternally aspirant, ... unpredictable because apparently without law; ... a law unto itself" (249). Although both Victor and Walton are at times aware that their quests are essentially compulsive, courses of action embarked upon almost against their wills, they both rationalize by stressing the intellectual and humanitarian values of what they are attempting to achieve. Neither considers that he is pursuing a dangerous and relatively useless course because of the sheer emotional excitement it affords him.

For Frankenstein and Walton, the exercise of masculinity follows a pattern so similar that the similarity cannot have been unintentional on Mary

Shelley's part. First, an interest established in childhood quickly becomes a burning, particular hunger—not for adventure in general, but for the adventure of discovery, of going beyond what had been thought possible or even proper for human beings to discover. Frankenstein expresses this hunger on three separate occasions as a "longing to penetrate the secrets of nature" (39; see also 40, 47). In each case, this ardent curiosity is established innocently—that is, without the boy's awareness of impropriety or error—but its establishment in both cases is due to a lack of (tamed) masculine guidance within the domestic circle: Walton finds only after devouring his uncle's sailing library that his father has forbidden him to embark upon a seagoing career; Frankenstein misunderstands his father's careless admonition about Cornelius Agrippa and supposes that his father has not really read what he has so easily dismissed. But both men, when they decide to follow their own inclinations, do so in defiance of their fathers' wishes. (This is true, so far, of Clerval as well, but Clerval will sacrifice his own inclinations, finally, to take the feminine role of supporting his friend, and will pay for this feminized masculinity, in the Gothic order of the novel, by dying at the Monster's hands. Clerval is often taken as a balanced figure after whom Victor should have modeled himself, and indeed he does represent the ideal—that is, the tamed— sentimental man. But his balance, achieved, as Victor tells Walton, through the gentle guidance of Elizabeth, only dooms him to share her Gothic fate.)

Both Walton and Frankenstein are offered a chance to avoid the doomed paths of their aspirations, Walton in his attempt to write poetry, Frankenstein in his brief interest in mathematics and physics. But neither is in strong enough control of his own destiny to take advantage of his chance. Both are kept in check so long as they remain in the domestic environment, but both escape this environment, and thus the taming feminine influence; as Ellis has shown, they must escape this influence in order to act according to their masculine wills. Both pursue their goals with some conscious awareness of the mysterious, compulsive nature of the pursuit, and of the desire for personal glory, but both rationalize what they do as being somehow for the great benefit of mankind, and both insist upon the rational, scientific character of quests that are in fact primarily irrational. (It is impossible to avoid seeing, here, that the pattern both Walton and Victor Frankenstein follow is that taken by Percy Bysshe Shelley in his defiance of his father, his pursuit of the imaginative ideal, and in his insistence—as in his "Defence of Poetry"—upon the practical, social good to be achieved by that pursuit.)

The various outcomes of masculine activity in *Frankenstein* further undermine the sentimental ideal of masculinity. While the feminine characters achieve their own destruction by passively complying, or appearing to comply, with the role assigned to them, the masculine characters fare little better. Everything Victor Frankenstein's father does, from his rescue of

Caroline to his urging of Victor and Elizabeth to marry, turns out to have been an active step toward the destruction he finally encounters. Henry Clerval, who forsakes his own ambition to become a kind of nurse and companion to Victor, is in Victor's eyes (that is, in the eyes of the sentimental tradition) a perfect masculine figure, having been softened and gentled by the guiding hand of Elizabeth; in fact, he has been so depleted that he has become another passive victim of the Monster. Interestingly enough, Clerval is not killed while engaged in the active task of traveling, but while he is waiting for Victor to complete the Scottish tour (an excuse for attempting to create the female Monster) alone, having been overruled in his objections to the separation.

Victor's compulsive action, throughout the course of his life, results in all instances (except in his final intention to destroy the Monster) in the successful accomplishment of what he sets out to do—and that success in every case dooms his loved ones to suffering and death. Walton alone does not accomplish disaster by his actions, and that is only because he turns back from his masculine course to pursue no course at all: his voyage back to England is a retreat, necessary after what he has learned from Victor and the Monster, but still a retreat into the tamed existence he now seems to seek. Thus we will not see Walton in his return to England, but we can guess that his return will be at least a disappointment; for one of the underlying truths of this novel—and of the Gothic in general—is that the two opposing ideals of masculine ambition and domesticity can never be truly reconciled in the perfect or tamed masculine man. Pure masculinity or femininity, unmixed as it must be in each individual, leads always to the fatal excess depicted by the Gothic. And the prescribed union of the two within the domestic circle must always be a failure, as Victor and Elizabeth's marriage is a failure, invaded by the Gothic excess of the Monster and the murdered bride.

Frankenstein is an antisentimental novel as it is told from the points of view of the two protagonists whose lives are dominated by their acceptance and pursuit of the sentimental ideal, and made ironic by contrasts between the sentimentally colored perceptions of Frankenstein and Walton and the reality they unwittingly reveal to the reader. Like Charlotte Brontë in *Jane Eyre,* Mary Shelley in *Frankenstein* sets up situations, characters, and values in order to subvert them, demonstrating the fallibility of the sentimental world view; like Thackeray in *Vanity Fair* she turns the reader's expectation of a comedic, sentimental resolution into a realization that the code of sentiment, carried on its own terms to its inevitable conclusion, leads to a resolution disappointing and unfulfilling for the protagonists. However, the two sentimental points of view and the reader's ironic, antisentimental perception of them are completed by a third. Because of this, Mary Shelley is able to go beyond ironic commentary upon the sentimental tradition, to show that tradition as the incomplete half of a divided, self-defeating, essentially tragic whole.

The Gothic Vision: The Monster and the Murdered Bride

To understand *Frankenstein*'s mirroring of both sides of the sentimental/ Gothic myth, we must recognize that it is indeed a Gothic novel. James Rieger's contention that it is not Gothic, in the introduction to his edition based on the 1818 edition, rests on the realism and immediacy of the book's setting, the concrete starkness of Mary Shelley's descriptive passages, and apparently on the fact that Frankenstein is not Radcliffian either in tone or in strategy; Rieger implies that to be called Gothic *Frankenstein* would need to be a romance, which it is not. However, even Rieger agrees that it has "affinities" with the Gothic tradition, and what he sees as a "reversal of the Gothic strategy" (xxvii) is actually an ironic revelation of the close relationship between the Gothic and the sentimental and of the nature of this relationship. Whereas Radcliffe and M. G. Lewis, with whose "romances" Rieger attempts to contrast *Frankenstein*, transport their sentimental characters into exotic settings to depict the confrontation between the individual and his apparently alien self, Mary Shelley heightens the drama of this confrontation and at the same time reveals its nature more truly by bringing the alien element into the familiar settings of the characters' lives. By drawing the stark, barren wasteland of the Arctic Circle, rather than a warm Italian landscape, as her metaphor for the heart's wilderness, she shows more clearly the nature of the country into which the Gothic and the sentimental pursue each other, the blasted sterility and frozen immobility that surround and spread outward from the cleft in consciousness that divides them from each other.

Furthermore, *Frankenstein* acknowledges that the Gothic terror is not of the Catholic south, nor of medieval times, but is specifically a feature of Puritan-influenced, middle-class, contemporary Europe. Geneva, traditionally associated with the Reformation and with republican enlightenment, but described by Madame de Staël's biographer J. Christopher Herold as a "society...tightly closed" whose government had "by the eighteenth century fallen into the hands of a jealous oligarchy" and where a "rigid class system" and stiff-necked Puritan morality dominated its citizens' lives (5), is a perfect setting for the ironic antisentimental aspect of *Frankenstein*. To show the split between the sentimental and the Gothic, and the relationship between the Gothic and the enlightened age in which it was born, *Frankenstein*'s setting changes in swift, dreamlike movements from Geneva to the medieval university town Ingolstadt to the wasteland polar ice fields. The blazing whiteness of the Arctic, characterized by Walton in the 1818 edition of *Frankenstein* as a place of "eternal light" (Rieger, 9–10), symbolizes powerfully the Gothic extreme of the Enlightenment—as the "whiteness of the whale" will do in *Moby Dick*. The white light of the region, where all colors are present and none is discernible, is suggestive of Shelley's vision of the Ideal, or "intense inane."

Walton's letters to his sister are dated "17––," but must have been written after the 1798 publication of *Lyrical Ballads,* for Walton quotes Coleridge's "Ancient Mariner" in one letter. The two-year period between 1798 and 1800 is obviously too short a time for Walton to have been inspired by Coleridge, tried the writing of poetry and given it up, acquired training as a sailor, and prepared for his journey toward the North Pole; thus, we must recognize an incongruity in Walton's letters that is impossible to resolve. But it seems significant that Mary Shelley chose to write "17––" rather than "18––," which without being more specific than she wished would have provided a twenty-year period between Coleridge's publication and the 1818 edition of *Frankenstein,* but which also would have allowed the reader to interpret the novel as futuristic fiction, a mode she was later to adopt in *The Last Man,* but perhaps wished to avoid here to give Frankenstein a contemporary setting. The eighteenth-century date, together with the references to the poetry of Coleridge, places Victor Frankenstein in Geneva during the period of the Napoleonic wars and the general revolutionary upheaval in Europe; and although we are reminded only obliquely of historical events (by the DeLaceys' troubles in France), we are thus made aware of a link between the creature that haunted the Frankenstein family and the terror that haunted all of Europe.

In Stoker's *Dracula,* the monster—the Count in his castle—is waiting for Jonathan Harker even as the novel opens, and Harker is aware of his presence and of their inevitable meeting though not of the Count's nature or the disastrous events that will ensue. Likewise, the antagonist or evil force is represented in most Gothic novels as something or someone already in existence, outside and hidden from the protagonist until fate or the protagonist's unwitting actions bring the two together, as for example Matilda in her disguise as a novice monk is already known to Ambrosio before she reveals herself to him, and as the Wanderer has commenced his long career before those innocents who will be threatened by him, in Maturin's novel, are aware that such a person exists. In *Frankenstein,* however, the dark force that will destroy Victor and his friends is not a separate entity until the creation of the Monster as a living being, which takes place in chapter 5, a fifth of the way into the novel. It would not be correct, however, to say that the antagonistic force is not existent before the Monster's creation; the entire story up to that point, including Walton's letters and the first four chapters of Frankenstein's narrative, prepares us for and chronicles the Monster's development as a part of the protagonist, a force hidden within the light of the sentimental mythos by which Victor, like Walton, has been shaped, an inevitable Gothic potentiality.

The dream that inspired Mary, according to her 1831 introduction, to begin writing *Frankenstein* had been of the Monster's coming to life, and it was with this incident, described by the narrator Victor Frankenstein, that she commenced the novel. The incident is, in the 1831 edition of the book, retained in the first part of chapter 5, and it is indeed fraught with the strange power and immediacy of a nightmare:

> It was on a dreary night of November, that I beheld the accomplishments of my toils. With an anxiety that almost amounted to agony, I collected the instruments of life around me, that I might infuse a spark of being into the lifeless thing that lay at my feet. It was already one in the morning; the rain pattered dismally against the panes, and my candle was nearly burnt out, when, by the glimmer of the half-extinguished light, I saw the dull yellow eye of the creature open; it breathed hard, and a convulsive motion agitated its limbs.
>
> How can I describe my emotions at this catastrophe, or how delineate the wretch whom with such infinite pains and care I had endeavored to form? His limbs were in proportion, and I had selected his features as beautiful. Beautiful!—Great God! His yellow skin scarcely covered the work of muscles and arteries beneath; his hair was of a lustrous black, and flowing; his teeth of a pearly whiteness; but these luxuriances only formed a more horrid contrast with his watery eyes, that seemed almost of the same colour as the dun white sockets in which they were set, his shrivelled complexion and straight black lips.
>
> For this I had deprived myself of rest and health. I had desired it with an ardour that far exceeded moderation; but now that I had finished, the beauty of the dream vanished, and breathless horror and disgust filled my heart. Unable to endure the aspect of the being I had created, I rushed out of the room. . . . (57)

The intensity of this passage results in great part, as Kaplan and Kloss note, from Victor's unexplained and unexpected emotional response to the success of his experiment. He has prepared the reader for it to an extent in the preceding chapter, describing his feelings of nervous anxiety, as his project neared completion, in terms of oppression, guilt, and neurasthenia. But the passage describing the Monster's awakening and Victor's response does nothing to resolve the tension between his obvious awareness of success and his just-as-obvious horror. The project, whch has turned out exactly as he has hoped, is described as a "catastrophe." Victor offers as the cause of his reaction the creature's hideous appearance. But not only is the creature's ugliness, as Victor describes it, insufficient reason for the overwhelming horror that suddenly affects him, but the reader must immediately recall that Victor has put the creature together himself and has been looking at it, imagining it alive, for some long time. There remains a thrilling tension between the momentous attainment of Victor's lifelong ambition and his wildly inappropriate response to that event; the tension reverberates through his entire narrative.

Kaplan and Kloss argue convincingly that Victor's horrified reaction is a sign of projected guilt at the fulfillment of oedipal wishes, and this explanation seems valid, especially in view of what Victor has already related about his feelings for his parents, his idyllic childhood relationship with his mother, and in view of the dream he will experience immediately after the Monster's coming to life in which his fiancée changes into the figure of his dead mother in his arms. But the more familiar explanation for Victor's reaction, implied in the subtitle ("Presumption") of the first dramatic presentation of *Frankenstein*, which holds that Victor's horror and guilt signify his realization that he has presumed against God in daring to create life, need not be rejected. In fact, these explanations do not contradict each other, as they are two ways of saying the same thing. Victor Frankenstein's reaction is a recognition and rejection of his own human nature, a nature incestuous and presumptuous, imaginative, creative, and murderous, contradictory and dark.

When Victor recognizes that the being he has created is alive, he recapitulates an ancient mythic event—the human being's recognition of himself as a creative creature (thus a paradox) and of the nature of his creativity. In terms of the sentimental/Gothic myth, the moment of the Monster's vivification, the victorious accomplishment that is at the same time a catastrophe, is the very event that stands at the center of the myth's dividedness. Given the nature of the sentimental/Gothic myth, its internal contradictions and its lack of satisfactory mythic distance, the creative accomplishment and the recognition of self that accompanies it cannot be accepted; instead, the moment contains creation and rejection at once, the irrevocable cleft in consciousness, the separation of the sentimental man as he must perceive himself from the Gothic Monster he must see always as his enemy.

If the Monster is the central Gothic element in *Frankenstein*, and his vivification the moment in which the novel's Gothic nature is revealed, still it must be seen that this is also the moment in which Victor Frankenstein attains his status as the perfect sentimental hero, the maturation he has both sought and resisted. To recognize Victor's nature and the nature of his conflict with the Monster, we must understand how the sentimental hero defines himself by the rejection of those qualities—Gothic qualities—he sees as unacceptable.

The ideal hero of sentimental literature, the potentially perfect embodiment of masculinity, in general appears as protagonist only before his perfect masculinity is accomplished. The struggle to accomplish this outcome, waged in the form of courtship and its complications, is generally the dramatic action of the plot, which has its climax at the moment that the hero accepts his domestication and rejects the possibility of becoming irredeemably, excessively masculine. The part of him that is monstrous is generally seen as somehow disappearing, being cast off from the perfect human being he has become. If this part of him is not defeated, then the character himself is seen as having become irredeemable.

Lovelace's rape of Clarissa represents his turning forever away from her offered redemption, and thus is the cause of her death—the inevitable fate of the Gothic feminine counterpart to the Gothic masculine monster. But Rochester's conquest of his own monstrousness—accomplished first by injury and blindness and then by his calling out telepathically to Jane—represents the *destruction* of the excessive masculinity that was the antagonist (symbolized by Bertha Mason) throughout the novel. Throughout the many variations of this drama, complicated by characters who represent various degrees of femininity and masculinity, the action is directed toward the attainment of perfect sentimental masculinity in the central male character, which will bring with it his domestication and the destruction of the monster he has contained. This is true whether or not the outcome is actually accomplished. The sentimental comic ending occurs when domestication takes place and the masculine and feminine characters are united; the sentimental pathetic ending occurs with the domestication of the masculine character happening too late, the feminine character having already died or having been otherwise lost to him. When the masculine character rejects domestication entirely, his story moves out of the sentimental into the Gothic—he *becomes* the monster.

The male protagonist of the novel of sentiment is interesting only as he is potentially either a perfect masculine figure *or* a Gothic monster. That is why, in those sentimental novels in which the male protagonist is memorable, he appears as a Byronic hero, capable (at least in the reader's expectation) of becoming either. His ambition, his desire for independence, his passion and bravado are the qualities that we find attractive in him, and these are the forces that must be successfully combatted by the feminine forces in the novel—his mother, his beloved, his already-domesticated male friends, and his own better self—for him to become the perfect masculine figure. When and if this occurs, he is no longer interesting because these elements of his personality have been extinguished. In fact, the novel of sentiment seldom shows him in his perfected state, because in this state he will have lost not only the qualities that have attracted his beloved, but also the passion that he has felt for her. Jane can tell us of Rochester domesticated, but we do not wish to see him that way; the idea of Heathcliff married to Catherine, settled into the life of a complacent farmer, is not only ludicrous but boring; Mr. B. and Pamela, after their marriage, are one of the dullest couples in literature.

In addition to his loss of attractiveness, the domesticated man of sentimental myth will no longer be able to function as a man in the world of masculine endeavor, separate from the feminine world of home and family. To show him continuing as an ambitious, passionate, independence-seeking male would be to admit that his domestication never took place in the manner asserted and prescribed by the myth. Thus Rochester must be crippled and blind, dependent upon Jane for his link with the world; thus Victor Frankenstein's father must be old, retired, passionless after his rescue of and marriage to Caroline. For the world view that so insistently separates masculine and feminine spheres of activity, there is no compromise both acceptable and believable. The perfectly masculine sentimental man is no longer recognizable as a hero. Thus the novel of sentiment must end with his appearance.

If, however, the struggle to uncover or create the perfect masculine figure is unsuccessful, then what emerges is the Gothic villain or monster. Our interest in him consists either in a fascination as he progresses from one depravity to another or in a sympathetic involvement with those characters who are threatened by him. Usually both sorts of interest are at work: Dracula, for example, arouses our sympathy and fear for his potential victims and at the same time retains the attractiveness of excessive masculinity, whether or not we wish to acknowledge its attraction. Melmoth, although we know or suspect that he is beyond redemption, so convinces Immalee that he is what she innocently takes him to be—the still potentially redeemable hero— that we are ourselves almost persuaded that he is not a monster. Ambrosio, who crosses the line to become a villain early in Lewis's novel, still appeals to us partly as a potentially redeemable hero (as his rejection of good is not complete until the final episode), partly as the excessively masculine monster that he is, and partly as he evokes our sympathy for his victims.

In either case, whether the sentimental perfection of the protagonist is accomplished or not (or if the monster, already existent, appears as a Gothic antagonist), the relationship between the feminine, sentimental, domesticating element and the excessively masculine, Gothic element that threatens domesticity is always directly adversarial. And whether the sentimental or the Gothic force dominates the action, the outcome is an exclusive victory for one or the other—at least, it is exclusive insofar as the plot of the typical sentimental or Gothic novel is concerned, although, as we have seen, the Gothic element is not completely destroyed even in those works, like *Dracula* or *The Monk,* in which the antagonist is apparently defeated; a Gothic potentiality, ignored by or unrelated to the plot, seems to resist eradication.

In fact, another outcome besides the exclusive victory of the sentimental or the Gothic element seems, however infrequently, to be possible. Whereas in a few cases (as in *Frankenstein,* with the survival of the Monster after Victor's death) the Gothic element appears to have triumphed, most Gothic novels and all but a very few sentimental novels (*Clarissa* is an ambiguous exception, with Lovelace's survival after the heroine's death) end with an apparent victory for the sentimental forces and defeat for the Gothic. Yet there is sometimes a suggestion, as in *Dracula,* that the apparent defeat of the Gothic element actually represents a reconciliation of the two opposing forces; the monster is apparently destroyed—by suggestively *erotic* means, such as the stake impaling the vampire—but actually becomes again an integral part of the sentimental protagonist. Such an outcome must be very well disguised indeed, as it is entirely unacceptable to the sentimental point of view, but it is subtly hinted in the references to vitality or fruitfulness (Mina's child, Jane and Rochester's marriage) that are said to follow the "destruction" of the monster.

All this is true, as far as it goes, of *Frankenstein*. Up to the point of the Monster's vivification, the novel's plot follows the progress of its protagonists (for Walton and Frankenstein must both be seen in this role) toward the point where they would, in a typically sentimental novel, reject—or be saved from— the potentially excessive masculinity that would destroy their potentially domesticated selves. Walton, when he encounters Frankenstein and the latter's narrative begins, is at a critical stage in his progress, for although we see from his letters that he feels an intense longing for the domestication his sister represents we also see him traveling further and further from it, the distance both literal and figurative, toward what, we do not know, nor does Walton himself. His moment of truth is significantly postponed until the end of the book, when after Frankenstein's death and the appearance of the Monster Walton decides to turn back toward England.

This might be taken as a typically sentimental happy ending, as far as Walton is concerned, except that we know—as does Walton, if he has learned anything from Frankenstein's story and the Monster's last appearance—that the powerful urgency that directed him northward will not be stilled simply by his decision to reject his dreams of exploration in favor of a feminized domesticity. We can have no great hopes for Walton's future happiness in England; thus, the end of the novel as it involves Walton is distinctly antisentimental. And despite what happens to Walton, the fact remains that he is overshadowed, the novel is dominated, by Frankenstein's tragedy.

Frankenstein's situation, as his narrative reveals it (interrupting Walton's progress until the end of the novel), is analogous to Walton's, up to the point of the Monster's vivification. Until that point the conflict seems to be a typically sentimental one, with Victor on one hand struggling to fulfill his masculine curiosity and ambition, and with his family (particularly Elizabeth) on the other hand struggling to curb and tame him. In fact, the successful end of his ambition—the creation of the Monster—seems to coincide with the successful eradication of it, his rejection of the creature. When he finally returns to Geneva there seems to his family and friends to be nothing but Victor's unfortunate but no doubt temporary melancholia, brought on by the apparently unrelated misfortune of William's death, standing between him and the required sentimental outcome, his marriage to Elizabeth. That the conflict is only beginning is apparent to the reader because of the novel's structure (Frankenstein has already confided to Walton that his story will end in tragedy), and is apparent to Frankenstein himself, who already knows of the Monster's guilt. Even then, the conflict is a secret between Frankenstein and his creature, with the young man's family and friends supposing that he is disabled by grief over the losses they have all sustained.

These disasters are seen by the sentimental element in the novel as unrelated misfortunes that should be countered by the domestic harmony and love uniting Victor with his father and his cousin/sister/fiancée. Only Victor perceives that they are acts of revenge by the Gothic creature he has brought into being, and that the creature's revenge is directed at his loved ones precisely because of his domestic ties to them. It is because Victor *has* been redeemed by the feminine force of domestic affection, has rejected the Monster, that the creature dogs him. Although he does not—cannot—explain why he turned away in horror from the being he brought into his life, he knows that if he is to follow the prescribed course of the sentimental ideal, to be Elizabeth's husband and his father's son, he must reject his creature.

In fact, Frankenstein knows that, in bringing the Monster to life, he is in effect rejecting it. The two acts are essentially one, for in creating the Monster he is creating himself as the perfect sentimental man, carving away from his conscious self the elements that are unacceptable to that role, externalizing them and denying them. His horror at the creature's first stirrings of life is thus not surprising: it is his reaction to the knowledge that he cannot disguise to himself, that his excessively masculine and "unmanly" qualities—the shadow or doppelgänger he had thrust from himself, the Gothic element unacceptable to the sentimental ideal—are as vital at least as the acceptable self that he consciously retains. The point is that, in the real world of this novel, as in the mythic world it reflects, the vitality the Monster represents will not simply fade away in the manner that the incomplete light side of the myth prescribes. In *Frankenstein*, the supposed victory of the forces of sentiment, the perfection of the protagonist as ideal, domesticated male, is revealed to be in fact the beginning of a fatal dividedness that will destroy both the sentimental world and the protagonist himself.

Plot conflict begins in earnest with this division, for to fulfill the role required of him, the character he has achieved in separating the Monster from himself, Frankenstein must continue to reject his double even as that double shatters the world they both inhabit, which is the conscious half-world of the sentimental myth. Even after the plot's climax—the death of Elizabeth—Frankenstein will continue the struggle, for once the creature has been created and rejected the only reconciliation possible is for Victor to accept what must be, to him, always unacceptable. Thus the irony of Victor's name—for Frankenstein's victory, his attainment of sentimental perfection, though it is certainly achieved, is the tragedy that will consume him.

There is a sense in which the novel *Frankenstein* should be read as a romance, a psychological metaphor, an allegory for the disintegration of

Victor Frankenstein's personality and for the career of criminal madness he embarks upon as a divided self. Such a reading is made poignant by the fact that it is Victor, the passive part of this double self, who narrates the story of both personalities but is only partly conscious, in a distorted way, of his own relationship to the criminal Monster, and thus only partly conscious of his own guilt. The irony of Victor's narrative is that he reveals to the reader the real nature of the relationship even as he conceals it from himself.

But to read Mary Shelley's novel as exclusively this sort of allegory would be incorrect, first because as a work of fiction it can be taken no further than itself. The character Victor Frankenstein may certainly be perceived, in a sense, as a madman who has systematically killed his brother, his closest friend, and his bride. But he may just as well be perceived as the person he consciously claims to be, the victim of a living being he himself created. In Victor's narrative, which is a part of Mary Shelley's work of fiction, both creator and creature are equally real. Further, we must remember that Victor's narrative is reported to us by another equally real fictional character, Robert Walton, for whom the Monster exists as a real being. And there is, in fact, still another sense in which both the Monster and Victor can be read as characters in a dream dreamed by Robert Walton, by which means his own unconscious mind warns him of the dangers of his enterprise of exploration and urges him to turn back.

To read Frankenstein's narrative as a psychological allegory, then, should not be undertaken as an exclusive or final means of discovering the novel's significance. But such a reading may be informative, clarifying and helping to reconcile other analyses of the novel, showing the significance of the divided myth in specific, individual terms. Above all it may demonstrate that Mary Shelley was well aware of the myth's nature and of its shattering effect on the individual psyche as well as on the domestic relationship that occupied a central place within it. One cannot read Frankenstein's narrative in this way without being struck by the ease, surely beyond coincidence, with which its details—especially the incongruities of the narrative—fit the reading.

Victor's Divided Personality: A Case Study

Victor Frankenstein's recounting of the incidents and general quality of his life before the creation of the Monster is significant in several ways. He dwells at length upon the circumstances of his parents' marriage and of the extraordinary devotion of his father to his mother, a devotion he describes in terms of "gratitude and worship . . . , reverence for her virtues" (33). The wide disparity in his parents' ages, he says, "seemed to unite them only closer in bonds of devoted affection" (33). His own early childhood he describes as "but one train of enjoyment" (34). The tone of his memories of an idyllic time to which he can never return suggests a glossing over of the inevitable small conflicts of domestic life to create, in retrospect, a perfect sentimental view of childhood. It suggests, too, that Victor recalls life as having been especially joyful while his world consisted only of him and his parents, before Elizabeth came on the scene—although this event, occurring when he was a young boy, is reported in the same idyllic terms, without a trace of the jealousy typical of a child at the appearance of a new sibling. (Kaplan and Kloss, whose psychological reading explores Victor's, but not Mary Shelley's, childhood, remark upon the probable presence of sibling jealousy. It might be noted that Mary herself was six years old when her family was enlarged to include a six-year-old stepsister, Claire Clairmont, whose presence she did not accept idyllically, then or later.)

In fact, while the tone of Victor's narrative of his early life suggests unalloyed harmony, love, sweetness, and light, some of his specific remarks about that time are at odds with this tone. His mother, who "possessed a mind of uncommon mould" and who had "committed herself to [his father's] care" at the time of their meeting, within two years rose from abject poverty to marry the wealthy man, many years her senior, who had rescued her after her own father's death. The elder Frankenstein thereupon "relinquished all his public functions" and devoted his life to her with "a show of gratitude and worship. . . . Every thing was made to yield to her wishes and her convenience" (32–33). During her husband's absence of one day, she found and adopted a little girl, obtaining his permission apparently after the fact. She presided over their home, although her husband must seldom have been away from it, a function that her adopted daughter soon came to share with her. (One is reminded of Mrs. Clairmont and Claire's dominating presence in the Godwin household.) Caroline took in another young girl, Justine Moritz, while her three sons were being reared; and on her deathbed, having insisted upon attending Elizabeth's serious illness at the risk of her own life, she in effect ordered the marriage of Victor and his adopted sister: "My firmest hopes of future happiness were placed on the prospect of your union," she said—had she planned to live with Victor and Elizabeth after her husband's death? "This expectation will now be the consolation of your father" (33). Victor's father, while he is said to possess an "upright mind which rendered it necessary that he should approve highly to love strongly" (33)—an interesting statement in view of his later occasions to disapprove Victor's actions—is seldom *shown* in the narrative as an active participant in domestic affairs or decisions; the language that Victor chooses emphasizes his mother's role and almost eclipses that of his father.

The picture that emerges is not the one Victor thinks he is conveying, but rather one of domestic bliss obtained by the expedient of everyone's "yielding" to Caroline Frankenstein's "wishes and her convenience." It is the picture of a stern, rather stiff-necked man in upper middle age manipulated by a clever young woman through a combination of strong-mindedness and affected martyrdom. The "show of gratitude and worship"—which, under the circumstances, might more naturally have come from Caroline than from her husband—is illustrated and illuminated by Victor's description of a painting that occupied a central position in the Frankenstein home. "It was an historical subject, painted at my father's desire, and represented Caroline Beaufort in an agony of despair, kneeling by the coffin of her dead father. Her garb was rustic, and her cheek pale; but there was an air of dignity and beauty, that hardly permitted the sentiment of pity" (78). Hardly, indeed! At the age of seventeen, Mary Shelley had eloped with a married man, in part to escape the long domination of her father's home by just such a woman. It is not surprising to find Caroline Beaufort's eldest son suffering, at her death and his entrance to manhood, a certain confusion in regard to the requirements of masculinity.

Victor's precocious scientific curiosity, interpreted by Kaplan and Kloss as a normal childish interest in the sexual mysteries of life (an interest to be expected in Victor, who was seven when his brother Ernest was born and in his early teens at the birth of little William), must also signify the intense need he had to identify himself with a masculine pursuit, one to counter the dominant femininity of his surroundings. He speaks of that interest as a "passion ... [arising] like a mountain river, ... swelling as it proceeded, [becoming a] torrent" (38), and says that it arose directly in response to his father's belittling of his first show of interest, at the age of thirteen, in the writings of the medieval alchemist Cornelius Agrippa.

Agrippa is, for several reasons, a figure through whom Victor Frankenstein could attempt to reinforce his masculinity. First, as Victor's language reveals, he saw the alchemist's "penetration" of the "secrets of nature" as a masculine enterprise. Second, by studying Agrippa on his own initiative and by continuing to do so after his father's expression of disapproval, Victor could quietly but effectively assert his own independence from his father in the approved masculine arena of intellectual activity. Third, by identifying himself with Agrippa, Victor could share in the alchemist's rebellion against the established religious and scientific authority of his time, a filial rebellion against paternal authority. (Ironically, Agrippa may also be linked with femininity and so with the future feminine endeavor of Victor to create life; one of the alchemist's writings was a Latin treatise on "the nobility and excellence of the feminine sex," mentioned in a nineteenth-century biography of Agrippa by Henry Morley, which was not published until after Mary Shelley's death. In view of her mother's feminist writings, of her own wide reading, and of Shelley's studies in alchemy and the occult, it is interesting to speculate that Mary Shelley, if not her protagonist Victor Frankenstein, knew of this link between Victor's adolescent preoccupation and feminism.)

Victor's language as he speaks of his scientific and quasi-scientific pursuits, as Kaplan and Kloss point out, is full of sexual double-entrendre; more specifically, it is markedly the language of a frustrated male sexual dominance. Victor claims to have had "a fervent longing to penetrate the secrets of nature" (39), and directly after speaking of "unveiling the face of Nature . . . [and] her immortal lineaments," he confesses to having "repined [at] the fortifications and impediments that seemed to keep human beings from entering [her] citadel" (40). At one point, when he recalls a temporary loss of interest in this otherwise consuming passion, he speaks of this change as an "almost miraculous" reprieve brought about, he thinks, by "the immediate suggestion of the guardian angel of my life" (he has already applied very nearly the same characterization both to his mother and to Elizabeth) and asserts that "her victory was announced by an unusual tranquillity and gladness of soul . . . " (42). This reprieve, however, was not to last, for at his departure for Ingolstadt shortly after Caroline's death he resumed his scientific curiosity almost immediately and more compulsively than ever.

What specific form his studies took he scarcely reveals, except that they were directed toward the creation of human life and that they involved a deep preoccupation with the human body and with death and its physical consequences. His discovery of the "astonishing" secret that was to result in the Monster's creation occurred, he says, as "I paused, examining and analyzing all the minutiae of causation, as exemplified in the change from life to death, and death to life, until from the midst of this darkness a sudden light broke in upon me—a light so brilliant and wondrous, yet so simple, that . . . I become dizzy with the immensity of the prospect which it illustrated . . . " (52).

In the very next sentence Frankenstein hastens to assure Walton: "Remember, I am not recording the vision of a madman" (52). But in a narrow reading of his account as the history of a psychological experience we must recognize that it may be, in fact, the "vision of a madman" that he describes, and that the sudden light that burst upon him in the midst of his contemplation of the body's dark secrets may have signaled the onset of true insanity. Although Victor as narrator looks back upon his youthful passion in pursuit of the mysteries of nature as a "torrent which . . . swept away all my hopes and joys" (38), he had obviously managed to persuade himself, during that pursuit, that he was fulfilling the masculine role expected of him, following a demanding but noble course. Even while he "pursued [the] undertaking with unremitting ardour" (54), neglecting to correspond with his family, he was "supported" by thoughts of domestic virtue, of "a new species [that] would bless me as its creator and source," of in effect fathering "many happy and excellent natures . . . " (54).

When his father wrote to him in reproach for his neglect, he says, "I then thought that my father would be unjust if he ascribed my neglect to vice, or faultiness on my part . . . " (55). So, while comforting himself with the thought that he pursued a worthy goal, he managed by dint of great effort and through terrible anxiety to thrust from himself those qualities that he must not recognize and acknowledge as his own, the passion and vitality, the masculine impulses he perceives as gross and excessive, the feminine traits inadmissible in his ideal (sentimentally masculine) self—and above all, the hostility he had suppressed against his feminine-dominated family. For a terrible moment he recognized that conglomerate of qualities as a still-living, still-vital, separate being, and he saw it "objectively" as a horrifyingly hideous Monster. Then he retreated, as he would after future moments of recognition, into sleep—and dreamed that he was embracing Elizabeth, who turned swiftly and inexplicably in his arms into the corpse of his mother.

Why should Victor Frankenstein have been driven to the extreme of madness, and why should his madness have taken the form of a monster whose actions, despite Victor's efforts to separate himself entirely from his creature, were directed at the destruction of William, Henry Clerval, Elizabeth, and indirectly of Justine and his father? If we pursue this reading of Victor's narrative as a homicidal madman's rationalized explanation of his own acts, his dream supplies a clue. The oedipal desires seen by Kaplan and Kloss in Victor's narrative plainly had as their object Caroline, and, as her surrogates, both of the young women identified with her, Elizabeth and Justine.

Elizabeth Lavenza was Victor's betrothed, and would seemingly have been the natural object of his sexual desire, sublimated only in the degree that the sentimental code required of a young man toward the pure woman he was to marry—a degree of sublimation which, as we have seen, was difficult enough in itself. But Elizabeth and Victor's betrothal, which seems rather to have been Caroline's idea than that of the young couple, was complicated by a relationship that, together with Victor's already strong identification of Elizabeth with his mother, was quite likely to have made their union as unthinkable to him as it was seemingly unavoidable. Although he calls her cousin, he had thought of her as his sister since they were small children. But, as he would later admit to his father, when the old man wondered if the closeness of the adoptive relationship was what kept Victor from going through with their marriage, he felt both a brotherly and a loverlike passion—an incestuous passion—toward her; "I never saw any woman who excited, as Elizabeth does, my warmest admiration and affection" (151).

In the 1818 edition of *Frankenstein*, Elizabeth is the orphaned child of Alphonse's sister; in the 1831 edition Mary Shelley eliminated the actual blood relationship, though Victor and Elizabeth still address each other as cousin. One can see no obvious reason for this change, as marriage between first cousins was not uncommon at the time. Victor's dream, the fact that the two still call each other cousin, and Alphonse's question about the relationship all indicate that Mary wished the idea of incest to be retained; perhaps she felt that Victor's psychological perception of the relationship as incestuous was more notable if the actual relationship as cousins did not exist. In any case, if one reads Victor and the Monster as two parts of a disintegrated personality, the sexual feelings of the young man toward Elizabeth have been displaced from Victor's consciousness into the Monster's murderous passion. This is strongly supported by the fact that all interest in the wedding night is on the Monster's, not Victor's, part. Small wonder that Victor both longed for and dreaded his union with Elizabeth, or that he attempted to widen the physical distance between them by imposing as well the distance of silence. But it was a letter from her—the first of two letters he quotes in his narrative— that drew him fatally back to Geneva and the situation he had tried to avoid.

Elizabeth's letter, received by Victor after his recovery from a mental and physical breakdown during which he was cared for by Henry Clerval, reminds him of his father's advanced age and of his own "duty" to return home so that his younger brother might enter military service—a reminder of obligation that seems contrived at least, especially as Victor had heard nothing of it from his father or brother. Elizabeth also takes several paragraphs, ingenuously, to "indulge" Victor "in a little gossip concerning the good people of Geneva" (66), which gossip consists of the news of three marriages within their set of friends, and of a charming description of his small brother William who, precociously enough, "has already had one or two little *wives,* but Louisa Biron is his favorite, a pretty little girl of five years of age" (66). As for herself, Elizabeth implies that she is gathering dust on a shelf, although, as she says, "My trifling occupations take up my time and amuse me" (64).

Were these pointed observations and reminders of his domestic obligations not enough, Elizabeth quite shamelessly devotes three long paragraphs to a discussion of her housemate Justine Moritz, of whom she says (after reminding Victor at length of who Justine is), "Justine, you may remember, was a great favorite of yours; and I recollect you once remarked, that if you were in an ill-humour, one glance from Justine could dissipate it . . . " (65). If Victor did not remember, Elizabeth certainly did, in precise detail. (And if Victor does not hear the implications of Elizabeth's long digression on Justine's cleverness, gentleness, and extreme prettiness, we may be sure that Mary Shelley, whose life with Shelley had educated her in the uses to be made of unavoidable triangular relationships, was aware of those implications.) Elizabeth, we feel, intended to handle Justine when the time came—for now she would use any means at hand to entice her fiancé into returning to his domestic obligations.

Her letter had the desired result, and Victor prepared to return. It was after his decision, based upon Elizabeth's letter, that news arrived of William's murder, incurred while the child, accompanied only by Justine, was playing in a forest. If the Monster, whom Victor knows intuitively to be the culprit, is indeed a fragment of Victor's own personality, then we can deduce that the child interrupted a secret assignation between his brother and Justine and threatened to reveal what he had seen. Surely this other protégé of Caroline's, not quite a servant but not quite a member of the family, was a safer object for Victor's inadmissible passion than Elizabeth herself, and we know from Elizabeth's letter of his attraction to her and can guess of her interest in return. Because Justine was in fact the main topic of Elizabeth's letter we may assume that Elizabeth guessed correctly that the reminder of this attractive young woman would more surely than her other reminders (of Victor's duty to her and his father and brothers) bring Victor back home. William's childish defiance and threats to "tell his father" (reported later in the Monster's narrative) are more appropriate reactions to the interference of a scarcely remembered brother in his own play with Justine than to the sudden appearance of a hideous, gigantic creature. Moreover, while the child's death was no doubt an accident (as the Monster will later tell Victor), only Victor's own guilt would account for his otherwise inexplicable silence in the face of Justine's conviction and imminent execution.

There is further evidence in the novel to support the theory that Frankenstein himself, acting under the guidance of the rejected or monstrous part of his personality, is the real murderer of William. For one thing, Victor's acknowledged feelings of guilt, which he attributes to the realization that he "has turned loose into the world a depraved wretch" (77), are in conflict with his resolution to tell no one about the Monster because of the improbability of his story; the contradiction makes sense only if he knows, unconsciously, that there is no objective Monster to be captured and found guilty of the crime. For another thing, only Victor's *objective* guilt would account for his allowing Justine to be punished for the act that he knows (unconsciously) he committed but is convinced (consciously) that he did not; his conviction of her innocence results from his conviction of the Monster's guilt, and if the Monster is not himself there is nothing to stop him from accusing the creature. Finally, only a tender and illicit relationship between Justine and Victor, complicated by her knowledge of his guilt and by her obvious dependence upon *him* to confess it, could account for *her* false confession, her inability to explain the evidence found on her person, and the astonishing scene in her prison cell, where she and Elizabeth wept in each other's arms while Victor "retired to a corner of the prison-room..., gnashed [his] teeth, and ground them together, uttering a groan..." (88). When Justine heard this, he says, "she approached me, and said, 'Dear sir, you are very kind to visit me; you, I hope, do not believe that I am guilty?'" He continues: "I could not answer. 'No, Justine,' said Elizabeth; 'he is more convinced of your innocence than I was; for even when he heard that you had confessed, he did not credit it'" (88).

This reading would explain better than any other several apparent lapses in the logic of the novel, including the problem of how the Monster managed to plant the locket in Justine's pocket without disturbing her. It does, of course, bring a similar problem of its own: If Victor himself came to Geneva without his family's knowledge, met Justine, and was discovered by William—a circumstance not wholly unlikely, especially given Victor's state of mind—how did he manage to return to Ingolstadt quickly enough to keep from arousing Clerval's curiosity at his absence? One answer may be, of course, that Clerval, accustomed to strange behavior during Victor's illness and convalescence, overlooked his absence in the turmoil caused by the news of William's death (Victor's narrative does not rule out an unexplained period of time between Elizabeth's letter and that of his father in which the murder is announced). A second, contributing solution to the problem may be found in the incredible speed and endurance of the Monster in Victor's description, abilities not inconsistent with the unusual physical powers sometimes evinced by insane persons.

The Monster's appearance to Victor in the mountains, and the creature's long narrative and plea for understanding, may be taken in this reading to represent the endeavor of the monstrous part of the divided personality to achieve reintegration with Victor's conscious self. Although this fragmented part of Frankenstein had violently killed a child, it had not yet become a deliberate murderer, and it contained—in addition to the violent passions Victor would consciously deny—the qualities of compassion, charity, vitality, sexual desire, and joie de vivre, the real, human strengths no longer available to Victor. The Monster's narrative explains, in a sort of parable, the contrast between these qualities and the ones acceptable to the sentimental world; it argues the usefulness of these qualities (as in the rescue of the little girl and the charitable activities undertaken for the DeLacey family), and it asserts the right of these qualities to be admitted into the consciousness of the world at large and into Victor's personality in particular, where they would be free of the suppression that turns them fiendish: "Make me happy, and I shall again be virtuous" (100).

But to Victor's conscious self, those qualities were still too horrible or shameful to be acceptable, and they were now irrevocably linked to the hostility he had suppressed with them; the deaths of William and Justine, though he already felt guilt in their connection, would have been forced into his consciousness completely had he accepted the Monster—that is, had he allowed the reintegration of his own fragmented self. Thus he rejected that reintegration, after promising a compromise (the creation of a female monster) that must be interpreted here as an admission of his own physical sexual demands, to which he would grudgingly yield in an effort to keep from more encounters with his terrible double.

But even the limited conscious participation in monstrousness that his promise required of him was too much for Victor to contemplate, and after long procrastination and a final desperate attempt to comply with the Monster's wishes (an effort undertaken while he was on what his family, impatient for his marriage with Elizabeth, saw as a sort of rest cure, a tour of England and Scotland with Clerval), Victor denied even that compromise to his antagonist. In doing so, he lost what small control he had retained over his monstrous double, and the creature continued its vengeful career by murdering first Clerval and then, after Victor's marriage, Elizabeth herself.

If the creation of the Monster is to be interpreted as the casting off of, among other things, Frankenstein's excessive masculinity—a set of traits that includes "gross" physical sexuality which cannot be admitted to the sentimental consciousness Victor's culture requires of him—then the Monster's demand for a mate may be taken quite literally. What Victor actually did after escaping Clerval in Scotland is reported very vaguely in his narrative, but it may be presumed in this reading to have been some attempt at a sexual act, one that Victor was unable to complete—not surprisingly, as he is no longer consciously the master of his own physical or emotional passions. The violence connected with this act (the tearing apart of the uncompleted female monster) was most likely not actual physical violence, as Victor himself committed it and as it left the violent Monster frustrated.

The killing of Clerval might be seen as an almost meaningless act of violence, prompted only by the terrible hostility of the Monster toward whomever Victor values, especially those associated as Clerval has been with Caroline and Elizabeth. But it may also be seen as a desperate act committed in an effort *not* to kill Elizabeth. Victor knew (from the Monster's warning— "I shall be with you on your wedding-night" [168]) that marriage to her would be fatal, and despite his effort to disguise from himself the meaning of the ambiguously worded threat, he knew that Elizabeth was in danger. After the killing of Clerval (which Victor would have been unable to accomplish consciously but which he would have allowed the Monster to accomplish in an attempt to spare Elizabeth), Victor was arrested and imprisoned. The only other persons ever to see the Monster took it, significantly, for Victor himself, and they accused him of the murder.

But his father, convincing Victor's jailers not so much of his son's innocence as of his status as a member of the *haute bourgeoisie,* came to take him back, still insisting on the marriage which Victor could not summon the strength, now, to avoid. His fate was in effect sealed by another letter from Elizabeth, in which she expresses the resigned belief that he "love[s] another" (187) and declares that, while she loves him dearly, she would be "eternally miserable" were he to "stifle, by the word *honour,* all hope of... love and happiness" for himself (188). The word *honour,* of course, doomed poor Victor to follow its dictates in spite of his terrible half-knowledge of the consequences, and he married his cousin-sister-beloved at last.

The dreaded wedding night found Victor still avoiding the consummation of his marriage, roaming the halls of an inn half-hysterically after cautioning Elizabeth to remain in her room. But her shrieks brought him back to her in time to see what no one else saw, the departing Monster, and what everyone else saw, his murdered bride—"her bloodless arms and relaxed form flung by the murderer across its bridal bier" (195). Victor's behavior, as he relates it in the passages directly following that describing the discovery, was distinctly that of a madman, and was apparently suspicious to those who observed him, who could find no trace of the fleeing murderer he reported having seen.

Mary Shelley, in corrections she contemplated between the 1818 and 1831 editions, changed the inn to a private house, apparently to make the Monster's appearance to Victor alone less conspicuously improbable. But though other changes contemplated at the same time (in the so-called Thomas copy of the novel) were carried out, this one was not. Why Mary Shelley made this change and then decided against it remains a mystery, but her doing so can only mean that she was aware of the problem and chose to leave the apparent coincidence of Victor's sole witnessing of the murderer's departure as it had originally stood. It is tempting to suppose that she wished to leave available evidence to support this sort of reading. Changes that she *did* carry out from the Thomas copy are incorporated into the passages describing the immediate aftermath of Elizabeth's death.

Victor's narrative makes it clear that the months after Elizabeth's death, which saw his own temporary incarceration and his father's death, were almost unreal to him; and after he "confessed" the Monster's guilt to an officer of the law—and was presumably taken for a dangerous lunatic—he escaped custody and "followed" his adversary to the barren reaches within the Arctic circle, where he was discovered by Walton, to whom he told his amazing story before expiring. (It should be noted that, like the Scottish witnesses, Walton saw the Monster at a distance, and he comments upon the size of the creature, although without other human figures or familiar objects to judge by he can hardly be depended upon to have made an accurate estimate. In addition, Walton held a conversation in his cabin, after Victor's death, with the Monster. This may seem to be irrefutable evidence of the Monster's independent existence; however, as the cabin was darkened and as Walton *covered his eyes* to avoid having to look at the Monster, it may also be evidence that Victor's death was really the termination of the conscious personality or its final submergence in that of the Monster.)

For all the evidence that the Monster is a repressed, unacknowledged part of Victor's personality, there is equally strong evidence that the Monster, an independent being created by Victor, committed the crimes that Victor attributes to him. Although this reading of *Frankenstein* as a kind of case study of a disintegrated personality seems to me as tenable as some other equally limited readings, it has the same obvious fault as those others; no narrow reading accounts for the richness of meaning so often remarked in this work. As David Ketterer says, "we have [in *Frankenstein*] a situation in which the Other does have tangible existence and can be both known and loved *at the same time* as one in which the Other is only an aspect of the self and both knowledge and love are forms of solipsism" (93; emphasis mine). It is important to recognize this necessary ambiguity; it is important as well that we admit such a psychological reading as one of the valid possibilities supported by this ambiguous novel, for only such a reading will explain several otherwise puzzling "flaws" in the book's logic and structure.

In fact, it seems quite possible that these so-called flaws, especially the apparent illogic of many of Victor's actions, were deliberately included so that such a reading might be suggested as a possible, but not exclusive, way of understanding the book. In all of Mary Shelley's fiction following her first novel, she was to be concerned with plausibility and accuracy. In *Frankenstein* itself she takes care to make the smallest detail of description precise and real, and to delineate the behavior and motivation of all characters except for Victor Frankenstein completely and believably. Only Victor behaves illogically; only his actions are expressed vaguely, with long periods of haziness or uncertainty; only his motives are ambiguous and contradictory. The behavior and motives of other characters may be to the reader apparently foolish or wrong-headed, but it is equally apparent that these characters proceed quite believably and consistently according to the logic of their own points of view. Even the Monster, if we accept his existence in the first place, is more real as a character than Victor. In comparison to all the other characters in the novel (as they are revealed by Frankenstein in his narrative, not necessarily as he perceives them), only Victor does not act according to a perfectly apparent logic; only Victor, as a character, is unrealistic.

Surely this weakness of the central character is a very great fault if it is not a necessary clue to the novel's meaning. But like other flaws seen by critics of *Frankenstein*, this apparent weakness is entirely consistent with realism and accuracy if it is seen as a revelation of Victor's character. Relating his own story as he must understand it, he is necessarily vague in regard to the passage of time, uncomprehending in regard to the appropriateness of certain of his own emotions and actions. He has rejected and become unconscious of the part of his personality that would explain those emotions and actions and account for the time he has "lost."

This reading explains, as well, other similar problems that critics have found in the novel. How does the Monster travel throughout Europe, cross and recross the English Channel, obtain a sled and dogs and provisions for an Arctic journey, without being evident to anyone but Victor, and how is he immediately available almost every time that Victor thinks of him? How is the Monster able to go directly to Elizabeth's room at the inn where she is murdered? How does he know Justine and Clerval by sight without ever having seen them or even having known of their existence? How does he happen to encounter, of all the small boys playing in wooded parks around Geneva, William Frankenstein? How does he happen to discover, of all the rural cottagers in the area through which he wanders, the very family able to educate him both in the literature of Frankenstein's culture and in the domestic relationships of a family of Frankenstein's social class? And why did Mary Shelley, who painstakingly edited and corrected a number of times before the 1831 edition was issued, choose to leave such apparent incongruities, especially those that might easily have been corrected, open to the criticism of her readers—if not to suggest that Victor and his Monster were, if the reader chose to admit the possibility, actually one person who at different times exhibited two different modes of consciousness, who saw himself as two separate beings?

It seems indeed probable that Mary deliberately left open the possibility of reading Frankenstein's narrative as exactly what Victor insists it is not—"the vision of a madman." Surely the possibility of Frankenstein's insanity occurred to her, as she has it occur to Victor when he assures Walton that he did not hallucinate the process of the Monster's creation, and also at the beginning of his narrative when he admits to Walton that, in any place but the wild setting around them, he would not expect to be believed, although he has no doubt that his story contains "internal evidence of the truth of the events of which it is composed" (30). Internal evidence is, of course, not shown—cannot be shown—for the actual occurrence of events as Victor tells them, for the death of most of the major characters and the abounding coincidences that Victor accepts unquestioningly have ensured that, of those who have had objective evidence of the Monster, no one is left but Victor. There is, however, much internal evidence, as has been seen, to suggest that the Monster is actually a part of Frankenstein himself, acting without his conscious awareness or volition.

Nor is such a possibility to be thought beyond Mary's experience or her powers of representation. Genuine cases of "split personality" are said to be rare, but such cases have been observed and documented. And there is little doubt that some cases of demonic possession, lycanthropy, and even the doppelgänger experience, reported in earlier centuries, represent instances of the same phenomenon. The presently accepted explanation of the phenomenon is, after all, simply a metaphor reflecting current beliefs just as were those other explanations. Mary's biographers agree that, even at the age of eighteen, she had been far more exposed to experience and the searching, stimulating discussion of experience than was usual for a young woman of her time. Her life had been lived among a radical, unconventional circle of acquaintances who were likely to have considered the phenomenon of madness an interesting and important subject. Moreover, Mary herself, as her work shows, was intensely sensitive to the nuances of personality even when her characters are presented as far less sensitive—see again, for example, Victor's first letter from Elizabeth and his less-than-acute comprehension of it. Nor was Mary without firsthand experience, if not of full-blown madness, at least of temperaments given to hysteria and hallucination. As her biographers make clear, both Shelley and Claire Clairmont repeatedly entertained visions of various sorts, sometimes apparently inducing them deliberately for the sake of the thrills thus afforded them. The idea of a split personality, or of a "vision" attaining a kind of objective reality, cannot have been either foreign or uninteresting to Mary.

Such a psychological reading of *Frankenstein* should be taken, then, as a key by which the meaning of this novel, and the nature of the sentimental/Gothic myth which is expresses, may be understood. It provides a metaphorical language that gives the myth in terms of individual experience. Through such a reading we can see, more clearly than through any other narrow interpretation, how the story of Victor Frankenstein and his Monster embodies what may be called the tragedy of the sentimental/Gothic myth in much the same way that the stories of Oedipus and Antigone express tragically the world view of the Greeks.

Victor and the Monster: A Gothic Tragedy

To Mary Shelley, the closest and most striking manifestations of the sentimental/Gothic myth—in its dividedness, in its disturbing impingement of mythic, imaginative terms upon the actual lives of men and women, and in its potential tragedy—must have been Shelley's works and the life she shared with him. Thus it may be seen that, while *Frankenstein* owes much to Shelleyan ideas, it is at the same time a cautionary criticism of those ideas.

P. D. Fleck, arguing examples of Mary's journal entries and her notes and introduction to Shelley's works, as well as analogies between some of these works and *Frankenstein,* makes a convincing case to support the contention that "Mary intended *Frankenstein* to be a criticism of the kind of idealism Shelley seemed to her to be espousing" (226). Surely the echoes in *Frankenstein* of *Alastor; or, the Spirit of Solitude,* written in the year before Mary began her novel, are frequent and striking, as Fleck, Small, and Veeder all point out. The *Alastor* poet's "infancy, . . . nurtured . . . / By solemn vision, and bright silver dream" (lines 67–68), his quest "To seek strange truths" (line 77)—like that of the poem's narrator, who "Gazes on the depth [of Earth's] deep mysteries" and hopes by questioning "In charnels and on coffins" to force "some lone ghost/ . . . to render up the tale/ Of what we are" (lines 22–29) are reminiscent of Victor's childhood and his adolescent quest. And, like Victor when the secret of restoring life flashed upon him, the Poet "gazed, till meaning on his vacant mind/ Flashed like strong inspiration, and he saw/ The thrilling secrets of the birth of time" (lines 126–28). The Alastor poet's rejected Arab maiden bears a resemblance to Felix DeLacey's Safie, herself in a sense rejected by Victor when he rejects the Monster. And when the *Alastor* poet "creates" the vision of the "veiled maid," for whom he will spend his life searching, his sight "by the warm light of their own life/ [of] Her glowing limbs beneath the sinuous veil" (lines 175–76) is strangely reminiscent, though its effect on the viewer is opposite, of Frankenstein's first sight of his creature stirring to life.

Further, at the moment of apparent sexual consummation between the Poet and his vision, "sleep, / Like a dark flood suspended in its course,/ Rolled back its impulse on his vacant brain" (lines 189–91)—as it does on Victor's consciousness, after the Monster's vivification, to bring him an incestuous dream. Like Victor, but more willingly, the Poet pursues his "vision" "Beyond the realms of dream . . . / He overleaps the bounds" (lines 206–7). And after being "ministered with human charity" by "cottagers" while he is on his quest, the Poet is seen "on some dizzy precipice" as a "spectral form," amazing mountaineers and terrifying children (lines 254–66). These images, especially in their phrasing, are strongly recalled in *Frankenstein* in images of both Victor and the Monster. There are other resemblances: compare "A gloomy smile/ Of desperate hope wrinkled [the Poet's] quivering lips" (lines 290–91) with the Monster's pathetic attempt to smile at Victor, and, as the Poet's boat is swept "with unrelaxing speed" into a cavern at what is apparently the end of the Earth, "The Poet cried aloud, 'I have beheld/ The path of thy departure. Sleep and death/ Shall not divide us long!'" (lines 367–69). His cry, addressed to the "vision" he pursues, is curiously similar in tone both to Frankenstein's declaration of revenge upon the Monster and to the Monster's farewell to the dead Victor.

Striking, too, are resemblances between *Frankenstein* and Shelley's later *Prometheus Unbound,* as Christopher Small points out at length in a chapter of his *Ariel Like a Harpy* devoted to a comparison of the two works. Small and Veeder both discuss specific resemblances between Victor Frankenstein and Shelley himself, beginning with the name "Victor," strongly associated with Shelley and his poetry, and including in particular Shelley's and Victor's similar fascination with science and necromancy and their similar sexual ambivalences. As Small remarks, many if not all of these resemblances must have been perfectly apparent both to Mary and to Shelley himself.

What may not have been so immediately apparent to Shelley are the resemblances between Frankenstein's disastrously successful quest and his own ideals expressed in much of his writing and in many of the actions of his life. For what Frankenstein succeeds in accomplishing, the "escape" of the idealized human being from the dark passions and forces that plague him (an escape that Frankenstein effects by externalizing those forces, but that he can never then make complete), is remarkably close to the freeing of humanity and the human soul from various earthly impediments that Shelley envisioned and sought.

As Small repeatedly demonstrates, Shelley's poetry from his juvenilia forward is replete, in imagery and theme, with instances of flight and pursuit—in many cases of pursuit turning into flight and vice versa—in which the protagonistic figure pursues ethereal, elevated truths or states of being, often through paradoxically dark means such as necromancy and necrophilia, and is in turn pursued by evil and sinister figures. As Small's argument shows quite clearly, the flight-pursuit motif in Shelley's work occurs as the expression of a division between dark and light, airy and grossly sinister elements, a division that echoes in all aspects of the sentimental/Gothic split in the consciousness of Shelley's century. Masao Miyoshi, in his analyses of Shelley's *Alastor* and *Epipsychidion,* has likewise noted this division, and regards it as "the Romantic paradox": the impossibility for the romantic imagination of encountering an actual Other (as opposed to the imagined idea of the Other, really the Self) without "relinquishing... 'shapership,' the creative... imagination"—that is, without relinquishing *self* (69–70).

This statement, in existential terms, expresses what much of Shelley's poetry (and, according to his and Mary's biographers, what much of his life), in his own romantic terms, seems to have had as a central concern: the division of the ideal from the grossness of the real, the division of the imagination and its products from the materials it must use and discard, the escape of light from darkness. The division, or attempted division, is a familiar one: it is the division of the sentimental from the Gothic, the attempted attainment of ideal sentimental masculinity, that the marriage between masculinity and femininity (but never the merging of the two) might take place. It is the attempted banishment of all qualities, of all conscious and unconscious human characteristics, that threaten the sentimental world view.

This attempted banishment is, as we have seen, never really complete, for the rejected human truths are embodied in the Gothic, which the sentimental cannot escape. In *Frankenstein,* the rejected truths, seen as inherently ugly and fearsome, are embodied in the Monster that Victor Frankenstein makes. In fact, the truths *are* inherently ugly and fearsome, because while they cannot be accepted by the sentimental consciousness neither can they be projected safely onto some distant mythic or archetypal plane. As the Gothic must always intrude upon the sentimental (as Melmoth must come to Immalee on her island and as Dracula must find his way to England), so must the Monster, once created and rejected, wreck Victor Frankenstein's domestic circle and his sentimental happiness. Frankenstein's tragedy is that he has done and continues to do what his culture requires of him; he has perfected his own masculinity, rejected the Monster of excess that is his own creature, the shadow he casts and refuses to recognize as his own. But as a perfected sentimental being, he is incomplete. He cannot escape his Gothic self, his doppelgänger, and, depleted of the qualities that it contains, he is forever at its mercy. As Miyoshi writes, "The common error of calling the Monster 'Frankenstein' has considerable justification. He is the scientist's deviant self" (84).

Like *Dracula, Frankenstein* is a Gothic parable of the self, both in its characters and in its structure. The novel is basically formed in three concentric rings: the Walton frame; within it Frankenstein's narrative; within that the narrative of the Monster. A different set of characters functions in each of these three parts, the characters of each set interacting with one another and with the two important characters who move across the boundaries of the structural rings, Victor and the Monster. Thus, the novel's structure helps to reveal Victor as a tragic protagonist as it reflects the inner, outer, and (in the Walton frame) universalized aspects of his character. (Richard Jennings, in *La Fenêtre Gothique,* argues that the concentric or labyrinthine structures of certain Gothic novels reflect the plot movement of classical tragedy. Although Jennings does not give *Frankenstein* as an example, his argument would seem to be valid for this novel as well, suggesting that such a structure may be intrinsic to the expression of certain mythic ideas.)

The central circle is the Monster's narrative. Here, itself framed by the history of the Monster's wanderings up to his confrontation with Victor, we have the story of the DeLacey family, the cottagers who unknowingly shelter the Monster and provide him with an education. In itself, the DeLaceys' story is very nearly a complete sentimental tale embedded at the very center of the novel, distanced from the reader by four removes; it is overheard by the Monster, who relates it to Victor, who in turn tells Walton, who at last includes it in a letter to his sister. There might seem to be little connection between this family's circumstances and those of Victor or Walton; however, several resemblances exist. The DeLaceys, like Victor's and Walton's families, are genteel, upper-middle-class people (though in reduced circumstances);

brother Felix and sister Agatha are bound by close ties of affection and are motherless, and Felix is engaged to a girl, Safie, who has been "adopted" by his own family. But there are at least two important differences. The masculine and feminine spheres and roles are relatively little separated or emphasized with the DeLaceys, and, as Kate Ellis writes, the DeLaceys seem in all ways to be less rigid, more truly affectionate than the Frankensteins. There is no "show of gratitude," no playing at "little wives," no picture of a martyred mother weeping over a casket, no required leaving of the feminine sphere to enter the masculine, no long separation punctuated by one-sided, reproving correspondence. The DeLaceys' domestic affection, as the Monster observes it, is apparently genuine, as the domestic affection Victor so strongly protests for the Frankensteins is apparently not. Another important contrast between the Frankensteins' domestic relationship and that of the DeLaceys is that Felix's sister and his fiancée are emphatically *not* the same person. Safie, though a Christian by her own mother's choice, is a non-European who must even learn her fiancé's language before they can speak together. And even in the brief portrait given by the Monster, it is apparent that she and Agatha are unlike in important ways (Agatha stays close to her father and brother, while Safie leaves her father to travel across an unfamiliar continent with one female companion as translator. When both young women catch sight of the Monster, Safie runs out the door; Agatha faints).

The Monster reports the DeLaceys' story to Victor exactly as he has heard and witnessed it. Having no previous conception of what a domestic relationship is or ought to be, he must at first describe actions only, and only at length report with confidence the emotional import of those actions. Unlike Victor Frankenstein, who gives a sugary, sentimental appraisal of his family but unwittingly reveals details that are at odds with that appraisal, and unlike Walton who professes concern and affection for his sister (and no doubt believes that he feels them) even as he deliberately arouses her probable fears for his safety on a voyage she had urged him not to make, the Monster tells of the DeLaceys' actions and words, his own actions and emotions, with absolute honesty. If the Monster has been seen as being more human than the other characters in the novel, especially Victor, it is partly because he is not "revising" himself and others according to a sentimental pattern that has been engrained in him. He reacts, first to the natural world, then to the observed lives of the DeLaceys, finally to the books he reads, in a truly innocent, unbiased way.

How, one wonders, might he have reported the life of the Frankenstein family had he observed *them* unseen over a period of several months? His reaction to six-year-old William, who will respond to him not so much in fear as in hostile, offended dignity (threatening to tell his father, the syndic), will unfortunately be murderous rage. His anger at Victor, who not only rejected him but made him hideous so that other human beings would reject him as well, seems justified. The family he has been observing has taught him that domestic love is expressed in loyalty. The actions of the Frankensteins toward others, in and out of the family, are characterized by effusive, self-sacrificial "service" that calls attention to itself and demands gratitude (as shown in Caroline's portrait) and by expressions of loyalty that are essentially self-serving and duplicitous (as in their allowing Justine, whom they profess to believe innocent, to be arrested and executed for William's murder). And Victor's actions toward the Monster have been, as the Monster knows, literally hateful.

Part of the significance of the DeLacey story, then, is that the Monster can attempt to make Victor see, through the contrasting behavior and situation of a family whose domestic affection is of a healthier, more honest, sort than that of the Frankensteins, the flaws in his own background and behavior. Beside this ideal family, Victor's real family shows up poorly, and his characterization of them as ideal can be seen as false. The Monster is in effect explaining Victor to himself by allowing him to see the real poverty of his emotional relationships—a poverty of which both his unintentional revelations and his very insistence upon their richness show him to have been unconsciously aware. (If we again for the moment regard the Monster as a part of Victor's personality, then we may say he is attempting here to bring to consciousness the emotionally crippling circumstances that brought him to his present divided state: the rigid conformity to a stereotyped masculinity, the necessity, in view of his culturally enforced ideals and assumptions, of his both seeking and attempting to avoid a basically incestuous sexual fulfillment.)

We must remember that the Monster tells his story to Victor *after* the deaths of little William and Justine, while Victor is in an almost suicidal state of guilt and loneliness. If we see the Monster as part of Victor (or if we view the novel, as Philip Stevick would have us do, as a dream telling), then we may see the entire DeLacey story—including the family's final cruel rejection of the Monster—as an attempt not to rationalize but actually to understand the rage and alienation that led to these deaths.

What the Monster asks of Victor is his compassion and his *control;* Victor is rightly, as the Monster says, his "natural lord and king" (100); if Victor will deal justly with him, allow him to serve his master, the Monster will be happy. Victor's creature recognizes his own nature, his strength, his potential destructiveness, but also his potential goodness. He knows that he is hideous and does not doubt that this has caused all the human beings he has encountered to hate and fear him (with the exception of the blind DeLacey, whose blindness like that of Tiresius may be taken as a sign of insight and wisdom, though the old man has no power to sway his more conventional children from their fear and hate). But, says the Monster, he could be benevolent if Victor would accept him with justice, if not with "clemency and affection"; he promises to "keep no terms with [his] enemies" (100)—but, he implies, if Victor will treat him well he will have no other enemies. He does not promise to control Victor, but rather to be subject to him. All of this is to no avail.

Victor, as he will admit to Walton, feels only such feeble compassion and curiosity as allow him to listen to the Monster's story. But the fact is that he is unable to deal justly, let alone kindly, with his creature. In creating the Monster he has deprived himself of the qualities the creature represents—true compassion and true forgiveness among all the rest. To continue in the role he himself has tragically chosen (a role he must continue to choose, if he is to remain himself a sentimental hero), Victor must continue to reject his creature even when that rejection assures his own continued misery and guilt. As he tells the Monster, "You have left me no power to consider whether I am just to you, or not" (101). The statement is all too literally true.

The Monster's narrative of the DeLacey family is thus a parable, on both a literal and figurative level, intended to instruct Victor and to warn him of the consequences if he continues to treat his creature as his enemy. It is also a Gothic tale set at the very center of Victor Frankenstein's narrative. As such it is both a conventional tale of terror, albeit told from an unconventional point of view, and an ironic mirror image of the conventional Gothic story.

To see the DeLacey story in the first sense, as a conventional tale of terror, we need only imagine its being told from Felix DeLacey's point of view. Though somewhat lacking in dramatic intensity (for the DeLaceys are rather improbably unaware of the Monster's presence, although they know that someone has been doing them small favors by stealth), it is still the story of an encounter with a monster so terrifying that the family must leave their present cottage and begin life anew elsewhere as best they can. Felix sees the Monster as a horrible threat to his family, and he reacts in fear and with violence, as all sentimental protagonists must react to the Gothic darkness as it suddenly appears before them. For no matter how ideal the love that has nurtured Felix, enabling him even to sacrifice his safety and well-being out of justice and compassion for a stranger (the Mohammedan Turk, Safie's father, whose escape from prison Felix arranged, causing his own family to be exiled), this love will turn back in horror in the face of the Gothic monster, the ultimate Outsider.

Inherent in the Monster's very existence is the paradox: his creation and his rejection are at once the same act. As the Monster will imply in comparing himself to Adam in Milton's *Paradise Lost,* he was made for a very different reason than was Adam. God created humanity out of abounding goodness, in His own image and therefore beautiful and good. Victor Frankenstein, creating a being in *his* own image, necessarily acted out of what he himself saw as evil and ugly; thus the Monster is precisely what his maker despised and feared within himself. He is hideous because Frankenstein made him, and Frankenstein made him—separated him from himself—because he was hideous. Thus he will remain hideous to everyone in Victor Frankenstein's world, the world of sentiment. In the few instances throughout Gothic literature of a monster or Gothic antagonist's being accepted by a sentimental protagonist, such acceptance is always the result either of a literal or figurative blindness on the part of the protagonist or of an innocence (like that of Immalee in *Melmoth the Wanderer*) as profound as the Monster's own. Once such blindness is removed or such innocence repaired, the acceptance of the Gothic by the sentimental is withdrawn.

It is significant that Felix's kindness to the Turk was itself not entirely an act of disinterested charity or regard for justice, but was at least partly motivated by his attraction to Safie and his hope that they would be married. The sentimental myth seeks completion within itself, through the domestic joining of masculinity and femininity as it defines those qualities. But such a completion, even when the sentimental ideal is very nearly realized, as it is in the DeLacey's case, can never be total. In fact, the more nearly it approaches the sentimental ideal, the more immediately and violently must the light side of the myth reject the Gothic as a threat to itself. Thus Felix, in driving the Monster away, is acting exactly as he *must* act in his role of sentimental protagonist, and helps in a sense to create the Monster as a Gothic force, bringing Victor Frankenstein's creature a long step closer to the enraged murderer who will culminate his career with the murder of Elizabeth.

The ironic telling of this Gothic tale from the Monster's point of view allows it to be seen also as a sort of mirror image or photographic negative of the Gothic. To the Monster, he himself is the protagonist, one who came to the DeLaceys in absolute innocence and potential goodness and was there educated in the ways of the world he has entered—a world in which the sentimental ideal is attractive but doomed by its essentially hypocritical incompleteness. He no sooner learns to appreciate and love the DeLaceys for their affection and loyalty to each other than he realizes how they have been driven into exile and poverty, because of those very qualities, by a world that professes to honor those qualities.

He learns, from the three books he has found, something about the imperfections of the world he has entered. Goethe's *Sorrows of Young Werther* moves him with its description of "gentle and domestic manners" and the "divine" character of its hero, but the differences between himself and that sentimental hero puzzle him, and from the book he learns "despondency and gloom" and weeps at Werther's "extinction... without precisely understanding it" (128). From Plutarch's *Lives* the Monster comes to "admire and love the heroes of past ages," to love virtue and abhor vice, and to "admire peaceable lawgivers" (129). But he realizes even then that there is another side to human history, that perhaps had he been influenced instead by a soldier's point of view he might have come to admire war and violence. And from *Paradise Lost* he then learns to contrast his own state unfavorably with that of Adam: the contrast is made complete when he studies Frankenstein's journal of his creation and its "disgusting circumstances." "Accursed creator!" he cries to Victor; "Why did you form a monster so hideous that even *you* turned from me in disgust?" (130).

Finally, the Monster learns, from his own unfortunate reception by the family he has come to call his protectors, that the world of sentiment he has come to love and admire is one he can never inhabit. In one moment he and Felix confront each other, and it is Felix who is the monster: "Felix darted forward, and with supernatural force tore me from his father, to whose knees I clung [in supplication]; in a transport of fury, he dashed me to the ground . . ." (135). Thus he learns from the ideal man of sentiment the excess in which he himself will dominate Victor Frankenstein's life. The sentimental and the Gothic are at that moment mirrored in each other, doppelgängers in a relationship that can end only in the tragic destruction of both.

Surrounding the Monster's story—or, more accurately, including that story, as it is reported by Frankenstein in the Monster's words, at its center—is Victor Frankenstein's narrative. (In both the 1818 and the 1831 versions, the Monster's six chapters of directly quoted narrative occupy a position practically in the exact center of the Frankenstein narrative. This physical location of the Monster's story suggests that Mary intended it to be central in the figurative sense to Victor's narrative, that she intended the life of the Monster to be seen as central to Frankenstein's life [both stories are complete autobiographies], and that the novel is much more carefully planned and professionally structured than many critics have been willing to admit.) As we have already seen, Victor's narrative may be taken either as a literal relation of actual events or as a "madman's tale" describing in distorted and often hallucinatory terms the experience of a fragmented personality. In fact, it should probably be taken, as the fictional form allows and as its artistic richness demands, as both of these things. In any case, Victor's narrative, which is usually thought of as the main part of this novel, deserves further close attention to several of its particulars.

On its surface the narrative is straightforwardly an autobiographical account of Victor's life from his birth (indeed, from before that, for it begins with a history of his parents', especially his mother's, lives) up to the time of its telling. This autobiographical form is interesting and significant when one considers Frankenstein's audience and his reasons for telling the story. He had resolved, he says in introduction, "that the memory of these evils should die with [him]" (29), but after meeting Walton and learning the explorer's purpose, he changes his mind and decides to tell his story to this man who is like himself in so many ways. He tells Walton:

When I reflect that you are pursuing the same course, exposing yourself to the same dangers which have rendered me what I am, I imagine that you may deduce an apt moral from my tale; one that may direct you if you succeed in your undertaking, and console you in case of failure. (30)

Three points should be noted in regard to Victor's decision. First, Frankenstein perceives his undertaking and Walton's as "the same course," fraught with "the same dangers." This suggests, since their specific purposes have been quite different—Frankenstein's the creation of a living being, Walton's the discovery of a polar continent or navigational route—that Victor believes a certain *class* of endeavor brings with it a certain *class* of danger. Walton's purpose can hardly be expected to result in the literal creation of a monster; thus, Frankenstein must see another type of possible disaster as a danger analogous to the one he encountered. He expects that Walton will be alive, whether he succeeds or fails at his endeavor, to profit from an "apt moral"; more important, while Victor hopes that his story will console Walton if the explorer fails, he believes that Walton's *success* may result, as his own did, in a kind of personal catastrophe, but one that might be averted if Walton accepts the "direction" of his story.

The second point to be noted here is that Frankenstein has recognized a similarity between his quest and Walton's not from Walton's specific explanation of his undertaking but from his evinced attitude toward it, from the explorer's avid single-mindedness, his willingness to "sacrifice [his] fortune, [his] existence, [his] every hope... for... dominion... over the elemental foes of our race" (28). It is not the quest itself but the obsessive determination to succeed in it that Frankenstein sees as dangerous—for he has listened with interest and sympathy to Walton's plans until the explorer begins to speak of his "burning ardour" to achieve them, at which point Victor bursts out: "Unhappy man! Do you share my madness?" Even then, before he will confide in Walton, Frankenstein asks the explorer to tell him "the history of [Walton's] earlier years" (28), and it is this history that makes him decide to tell his own story.

Finally, in light of the fact that Frankenstein perceives his and Walton's ventures as being alike because of their like attitudes toward the ventures, a third important point to be drawn from his expressed purpose in telling Walton his story is this: Victor believes that he must tell Walton not only of his experiment and its disastrous success, but also of his entire life and family history. All this can mean only one thing—that Frankenstein, consciously or not (and "sanely" or not), considers his misfortunes and Walton's dangers as resulting from, as being in fact part of, the lives they have led since birth. He

finds in their lives, their directions, their characters, an essential sameness that
will lead to success in the undertaken venture and that will bring, with success,
disaster (a disaster that is inevitable if Walton does not act according to the
"apt moral" of Frankenstein's story). And as we have seen, the *sameness* of
Walton and Frankenstein is their mutual glorification of domestic felicity at
the same time they flee the feminine confines of such felicity to pursue with
compulsive energy excessively masculine ideals. They are alike in their mutual
participation, to potentially tragic effect, in the sentimental/Gothic myth.

That the situation of the sentimental protagonist is at least potentially
tragic may be seen when we reflect that this sort of character is required—
indeed, is "fated"—by his world view, the sentimental tradition that informs
his life, to pursue at all cost a course that will, if he succeeds, bring him
inevitably to disaster. By their very nature, the virtues he exhibits bring him
closer and closer, as he approaches the ideal state of virtuousness upheld by
his culture, to that division by which his culture is marked. The more noble the
character of the sentimental hero, the greater will be his drive to achieve
perfect, i.e., domesticated, masculinity and to eradicate from himself not only
the excesses of what his culture sees as masculinity but also the traits within
himself that it sees as feminine; and at the same time he will struggle as
determinedly to benefit from those feminine traits through uniting himself
with the accepted embodiment of them. Such a character will, in fact, pit his
whole strength against himself to reach a self-contradictory goal that he will
not see as divided. A sentimental protagonist who is truly heroic, as
Frankenstein is, will not fail to achieve his goal—and his success will always be
disastrous.

That Victor Frankenstein is of heroic stature is asserted by Walton before
the Frankenstein narrative begins. In his description of the stranger he has
welcomed onto his ship, the explorer describes Frankenstein as a specifically
sentimental hero, in appearance ("his eyes have generally an expression of
wildness, and even madness; but there are moments when...his whole
countenance is lighted up, as it were, with a beam of benevolence and
sweetness that I never saw equalled" [25]), and in behavior ("He is so gentle,
yet so wise; his mind is so cultivated; and when he speaks, although his words
are culled with the choicest art, yet they flow with rapidity and unparalleled
eloquence" [27]). Frankenstein is the very person Walton has been longing
for, the one man to whom the explorer may give his true friendship, for unlike
the ship's officers of whom Walton has already spoken, Frankenstein is both
manly—possessed of the masculine virtues of courage and generosity (at least
apparently; it is interesting that Walton admires what Frankenstein must once
have been as opposed to what he is now)—and refined. But although Walton
judges Frankenstein's character, from his observation of him, as heroic
("Sometimes I have endeavored," he says,

to discover what quality it is that he possesses, that elevates him so immeasurably above any other person I ever knew. I believe it to be an intuitive discernment; a quick but never-failing power of judgment; a penetration into the causes of things, unequalled for clearness and precision...[29]),

it is Frankenstein's narrative itself that must reveal how ironically correct Walton's judgment is. In Victor Frankenstein's story of his disastrous life we see the human tragedy inherent in the dividedness of the sentimental/Gothic world.

The beginning of Frankenstein's story, in conventional autobiographic style ("I am by birth a Genevese; and my family is one of the most distinguished of that republic" [31]), establishes the protagonist's heroically elevated state in terms specifically sentimental. He identifies himself immediately as a member of the upper middle class and of a distinguished family in a city linked economically and religiously to the sentimental myth. He goes on to give the previously discussed account of his parents' marriage and his own childhood, an account highly colored with sentimental idealism. Thus Frankenstein begins to establish himself as a tragic hero of the sentimental/Gothic world by revealing himself to have begun in the highly elevated state of childhood—not so much of innocence as of a Wordsworthian supremacy, "trailing clouds of glory." The state of the romantic child, unalloyedly joyful in the as-yet-unbroken circle of its sentimental family, can never be reattained in adulthood. Part of Frankenstein's tragic fall is simply his growing up as an imperfect adult in a culture that forces him almost immediately both to conform to the incomplete role designated as masculine (as his small brother, described in Elizabeth's letter, will do) and to seek the completion of that identity in a domestic arrangement that can only approximate at best the glowingly recalled state of childhood.

In Frankenstein's description of his childhood and youth he makes it clear that the development of his character is inevitable, that none of the steps leading toward the creation of the Monster is taken by his personal choice. While we see his actions as volitional during this period, based on characteristic decisions, they are plainly determined by his situation in life and his character as that situation shapes it, and in telling his story Victor stresses that his development was fated. First he is "given" Elizabeth by his mother— as sister, cousin, playfellow, bride, and possession—at once his "better half" and the burden of frail femininity for which he will be responsible always, in that inescapable and contradictory relationship imposed by the sentimental culture upon a man and woman. Victor has no more choice in this matter than he had over the country and social class into which he was born. In addition to this relationship that is to culminate in Elizabeth's death (oddly foreshadowed in Victor's first discussion of her: "my more than sister, since till death she was to be mine only" [36]), Victor is given those other elements that will bring him to the destruction of his world: his "sometimes violent" temper and "vehement" passions, the "law in [his] temperature" that directs him toward the "metaphysical, or, in its highest sense, the physical secrets of the world" (37)—in other words, the masculine attributes that are potentially excessive, brutal, overreaching, until they are tamed by feminine influence—in Victor's case, until they are projected onto his brutal, vengeful Monster.

Victor points out to Walton each of the several instances that might have been turning points to lead him away from "the fatal impulse that led to [his] ruin" (39), but in none of those instances does he have the power of choice, given his original tendencies of character. It is chance that leads him to the study of medieval philosophers and alchemists, chance and ignorance that keep him from learning that their "principles...had been exploded" by "a modern system of science" (39), and chance again that brings him to "the subject of electricity and galvanism.... Thus strangely are our souls constructed," he tells Walton, "and by such slight ligaments are we bound to prosperity or ruin" (41). The "spirit of good," Victor believes, made one "last effort...to avert the storm that was even then hanging in the stars"—bringing with "her [temporary] victory...an unusual tranquillity and gladness of soul" by which he was "taught to associate evil with [the] prosecution" of his studies, and to associate "happiness with their disregard" (42). Despite this last effort of the "spirit of good"—a spirit identified as feminine and tranquilizing— "Destiny was too potent, and her immutable laws had decreed [Victor's] utter and terrible destruction" (42). The potentially excessive masculinity he is *destined* to find, indeed to stimulate, within his character, and to follow, while he is equally destined to associate it with evil, will be caught, externalized, and rejected in the form of the Monster. Frankenstein, superior to every other being in Walton's experience, the shining first son of an idealized sentimental family, is fated by his participation in the sentimental tradition to be "utterly destroyed," like the oak he has seen riven by lightning, by the attainment for which he strives.

What Victor Frankenstein sees, retrospectively, as fate or destiny—and he continually refers to it in those terms—we may choose to describe as predisposition or the force of environment or even, in Freudian terms, as the id exerting its urgent demands on Frankenstein's personality. In any case it continues to make itself felt despite his conscious and unconscious efforts to deflect it. After his mother's death, although he "obtain[s] from [his] father a respite of some weeks" (44), he is sent away from the influence of his family, from the "spirit of good" in the form of Elizabeth, to Ingolstadt where his fate will continue to force him closer and closer to disaster.

Here he will come under the masculine influence of the Enlightenment in the persons of two professors, one of whom, M. Krempe, scoffs at his outmoded pseudoscientific preparation but sends him to the other, M.

Waldman, who introduces him to the modern scientific writers and principles that will allow him to begin his great experiment. He is especially disposed toward Waldman, who with his fatherly "aspect of greatest benevolence" and voice "the sweetest I had ever heard" (47) is a model of sentimental masculinity to Victor. Waldman accepts Victor as his disciple and gives him decisive help along the road to his terrible success. "Thus ended a day memorable to me," says Victor to Walton, of the day of his acceptance by Waldman; "it decided my future destiny" (49). Surrounded by the masculine environment of the university and of modern science, deprived of the saving femininity of his home, Victor commences upon the last step of his tragic success.

As he begins his scientific study, two events—his attainment of maturity and his mother's death—are irrevocably mixed in his unconscious and are brought to the surface in what seems to him a reasonable course of study: "To examine the causes of life, we must first have recourse to death" (51). He speaks of his apparently willing pursuit of his studies in passive terms, as if he had been coerced by fate: "Now I was *led* to examine the cause and progress of ... decay, and *forced* to spend days and nights in vaults and charnel-houses" (51–52; emphasis mine). Almost immediately the secret of life is illuminated for him, and he is "surprised ... that [he] alone should be reserved to discover so astonishing a secret" (52). He begins work compulsively, seeing nothing of the "charms of nature" that the passing seasons bestow around him, and "forget[ting] those friends who were so many miles absent, and whom [he] had not seen for so long a time" (55). Carried helplessly by the wave of his own destiny, he builds the Monster and, "on a dreary night of November, ... [beholds] the accomplishment of [his] toils" (57).

From now on Victor Frankenstein is, in his own conscious personality (or, in his own telling, as a strangely depleted person, enervated by his horrible success in the infusion of life into his Monster), more than ever incapable of choosing the course of his life and certainly incapable of controlling the Monster. In only two more instances does he seem to have a choice, and in both of these cases his freedom of choice may be seen as only apparent; having created both himself and the Monster in the divided image of the myth of sentiment, he must go on maintaining the antagonistic relationship that is a part of the character of both. As Victor Frankenstein, the creator and victim of the Monster, he is no longer able to control his destiny in even the smallest degree.

The first instance when he might be said to have a choice is his meeting with the Monster after Justine's execution, on which occasion the Monster relates the long narrative of his own history and that of the DeLacey family. The Monster, passionately but reasonably, begs Victor to act with justice toward his creature. But Victor, as has already been seen, is incapable of such action:

"Why do you call to my remembrance," I rejoined, "circumstances, of which I shudder to reflect, that I have been the miserable origin and author? Cursed be the day, abhorred devil, in which you first saw light! Cursed (although I curse myself) be the hands that formed you! You have made me wretched beyond expression. You have left me no power to consider whether I am just to you, or not. Begone! relieve me from the sight of your detested form." (101)

While Victor acknowledges his own guilt, he places the blame for this guilt upon his creature. He is able to feel guilt and remorse, but unable to be reunited with the "devil" who, once created, has been the uncontrollable cause of his guilt.

The next instance in which Victor apparently has a choice of directing his own actions, and thus controlling the Monster, is the creation of the promised female monster. This he has kept from doing for as long a time as possible, but has finally nearly accomplished, having gained the solitude of "one of the remotest of the Orkneys" (163) during his visit accompanied by Henry Clerval to England and Scotland. He contemplates the loathsomeness and the unknown disposition of the being he is forming:

She might become ten thousand times more malignant than her mate, and delight, for its own sake, in murder and wretchedness.... They might even hate each other; the creature who already lived loathed his own deformity, and might he not conceive a greater abhorrence for it when it came before his eyes in the female form? She also might turn with disgust from him to the superior beauty of man.... (165)

Further, he thinks, the two—if they did not disgust each other—would produce "a race of devils ... who might make the very existence of the species of man a condition precarious and full of terror. Had I a right ... to inflict this curse upon everlasting generations?" (165). Motivated partly by disgust, partly by ignorance of the probable disposition of the female monster (for those excessively masculine qualities that made the first creature loathsome to him would be "ten thousand times" more dreadful in a female), and partly by his rationalization that he would be "inflict[ing a] curse upon everlasting generations" (note that his reasons are the same, only exactly reversed, as those he gave for making the first Monster), Victor sits immobile until— apparently summoned by his very thought of monstrousness—the original Monster appears at the window. "As I looked on him," says Victor,

his countenance expressed the utmost extent of malice and treachery. I thought with a sensation of madness on my promise of creating another like to him, and trembling with passion, tore to pieces the thing on which I was engaged. The wretch saw me destroy the creature on whose future existence he depended for happiness, and, with a howl of devilish despair and revenge, withdrew. (166)

Victor's apparent choice, as we may see, is no real choice. Especially as the perfect example of sentimental masculinity that he has become, having cast off from himself all those excessive traits that the Monster embodies, Victor is incapable of choosing even to give the Monster "the creature on whose future existence he depended for happiness." He has, in fact, by destroying the female monster, strengthened his first creature so that, besides being uncontrollable himself, the Monster now has control over Victor. "You are my creator," the Monster tells him now, "but I am your master.... You can blast my other passions; but revenge remains...!" (167–68). Now the thwarted Monster utters the threat that will be fulfilled in the death of Elizabeth. Victor has *chosen* his fate only inasmuch as he has chosen to be all that the sentimental myth demands of him. But his doom is sealed.

If Victor is destined, as a sentimental hero, to create and reject the Monster that will destroy his world, so are the other characters within his narrative destined—especially as they appear to Victor in their idealized sentimental roles, but also as they are required by their culture to live those roles—to act with him in the development and culmination of his tragedy. Insofar as Victor perceives them, his parents, Elizabeth, William, Justine, and Henry Clerval are, as surely as is the Monster or Victor himself, figures in a mythical sentimental drama. Insofar as he reveals them to the objective perception of the reader, they are realistic characters caught by their own necessities and cultural preconceptions and so forced to play the roles that figure in that drama.

Victor's parents are in some ways the ideal parental couple of sentimental myth, a man and woman so widely separated in age as to seem sexually incompatible (and thus, to their children, emblematic of the intense but bodiless passion required of sentimental love). Although we do not know why the elder Frankenstein has not married earlier in life, we may see that, as Kate Ellis suggests, his late marriage permits a separation of the masculine and feminine spheres inasmuch as he retires from one to give himself up to the other. (Victor tells Walton that his father "passed his younger days perpetually occupied by the affairs of his country; a variety of circumstances had prevented his marrying early" [31] and conjectures that "perhaps during former years he had suffered from the late-discovered unworthiness of one beloved..." [37]. Actually, as has been seen, a disparity in ages was not uncommon for a system in which men came late to their inheritance while women were of "marriageable age" for only a brief period in their late teens and early twenties.)

Victor's characterization of his father, whose "upright mind... rendered it necessary that he should approve highly to love strongly," is a somewhat wooden portrait, couched in terms much like those he will use to describe

Waldman, the tutor with whom he will have little personal association. If it were not for the characterization provided by the elder Frankenstein's behavior, as Victor relates it, we might dismiss him (and indeed all of the characters in Victor's narrative, with the exception of the Monster) as a stock sentimental character, poorly realized by the novelist. But we see him bestowing "gratitude and worship" upon the young wife whom he has rescued from poverty and illness, returning from a short journey to find an adopted child of whom he has had no previous knowledge playing with his little son, telling his university-bound eldest child that he will "regard any interruption in... correspondence as a proof that... other duties are equally neglected" (55)—and then making "no reproach in his letters, and only... enquiring... more particularly than before" into that son's occupations when the son neglects to correspond for half a year (56). We find Victor's father acting without any real power throughout the novel, succeeding only in nagging his son into a marriage that the young man is obviously unwilling to enter, then falling into a decline and dying after Elizabeth is killed. We are told that Alphonse Frankenstein had been a powerful and respected public man, but we find him in his private, domestic life to be a weak figure, dominated by his wife until her death, dependent upon and meddling into the affairs of his children until his own. His masculinity, exercised in his public career, has been exhausted, and his role has dwindled to that of a sort of stern, dignified figurehead for his son, who sees the sternness and air of dignity but not the empty ineffectuality behind them.

Frankenstein's mother, despite her early death—in fact, partly *because* of her early death—has a much stronger effect upon Victor. Although he sees her as the woman in the portrait, weeping over her father's coffin, and as the "fair exotic" plant in need of his father's protection, he reveals her as a strong-minded woman who controls her family's life to a great extent and is of tremendous influence on Victor (as his dream demonstrates) even after her death. Caroline Frankenstein seems indeed to be very possibly that sort of determined woman who appears in much sentimental literature as the strong, prop-of-the-family mother (as in Alcott's *Little Women*) and in antisentimental works (though often ambiguously—as for example Amanda in Tennessee Williams's *Glass Menagerie*) as the self-styled martyr whose affected weakness is her strength. From Victor's point of view, as we have seen, Caroline is the angelic figure who demonstrates perfect femininity, through her union with the "strong" man she has married, but who may not— indeed must not—carry any real influence into the masculine sphere outside the home. From what he unwittingly reveals of her, we know that she does have real influence upon Victor's masculine career, but that her influence is not for good, determining as it does Victor's unhappy and unwilling preoccupation with sex and death that ends in his creation of the Monster.

In the case of Elizabeth Lavenza (as in that of Caroline Frankenstein, though more clearly, because we are given more details about Elizabeth) the novel presents what amounts to three different but overlapping characters: the idealized, sentimental woman that Victor sees; the person that she pretends, consciously or not, to be; and the woman she really is. For the first we have Victor's descriptions of her, as his "pretty present" (35) from Caroline; as the "saintly soul [shining] like a shrine-dedicated lamp" in the Frankenstein home (38); as the brave, devoted "little woman" who "veil[s] her grief, and [strives] to act the comfortor" to her family upon her mother's death (44); and finally as the "bloodless . . . relaxed form flung by the murderer on its bridal bier," whom Victor at last embraces.

It is the idealized but confused sentimental picture, held by Victor, that makes Elizabeth's Gothic death inevitable. She is his promised bride and his sister, for whom he must and must not feel physical passion; his angel and comfortor, to whom he must defer, by whom he must be tamed and at the same time his possession—"to protect, love, and cherish" (35) in the sentimental ideal of love between fatherly man and daughterly woman. Thus Elizabeth, in Victor's sentimental perception, is especially that asexual being who is most attractive—because she is the recipient of passion but absolutely beyond passion—in her death. Given Victor's idea of Elizabeth, it is inevitable that their marriage will be consummated not by Victor but by the Monster, not in sexual climax but in violent murder.

However, Elizabeth herself, as a real character whose actions betray her affectation of femininity as a role, helps to bring about her own death and Victor's catastrophe. As Kate Ellis has said, Elizabeth is ineffectual in any of those situations in which she might actually have helped those whom she loves. Her courtroom appeal for Justine does no good, and her influence on Victor disappears completely when he leaves for Ingolstadt. On the night of her death she allows Victor to wander the halls watching for the Monster without herself knowing what the danger might be, although she must be aware from Victor's actions that there is indeed a danger. In only two instances does she actually accomplish what she sets out to do; these are the occasions of the letters she writes to Victor. In both instances Mary Shelley has her narrator quote the letters directly, thus allowing the reader to see "between the lines" the contrast between Elizabeth's real motives and feelings and those she pretends. And in both instances Elizabeth's effectiveness is disastrous.

In her first letter, begging Victor to return for the sake of his father and brother, describing little William's "little wives," contrasting her own "trifling occupations" with the marriages of her friends, and finally throwing Justine's attractions quite shamelessly before Victor, we see (as Victor does not) the attempt of a young woman in a difficult situation to do the best she can for herself without appearing selfish or unfeminine. Already affianced to Victor, she has no social life and no hope for marriage to anyone else. Her fiancé has been away for nearly two years, and now he has—after failing to write for several months—suffered and recovered from a mental and physical breakdown, the causes of which she cannot know. She is in the awkward position of living with and caring for her own adoptive father, who is her fiancé's father as well, whose fondest hope is for their marriage, but who is unable to bring that marriage about. She has received "many letters" from Henry Clerval (67) but not one line from Victor; she is understandably distraught, and it is understandable that pride and the role she has been taught to play will not allow her to write straightforwardly.

Her second letter, in which she tells Victor (after his incarceration for the murder of Clerval) that she will release him from his promise if he "loves another," is more direct but still devious and even more desperate. It must be obvious to Elizabeth that something has gone terribly wrong with her engagement to Victor, but she can have no idea what it is. She has no reason to believe that there is another woman in his life, but by backhandedly appealing to his "honour" in telling him not to let that virtue stand between him and his real love—whoever she may be—Elizabeth attempts to persuade Victor, in the only way that *she* honorably may, either to marry her at last or to free her from the engagement. Her very willingness to marry him in his apparent state of neurosis and reluctance reminds us how unhappy her circumstances will be should he "free" her now.

In writing both letters, Elizabeth is indeed effective, but the effect is disastrous to her: Victor first returns to Geneva at the death of William and the trial of Justine for murder; in the second instance he gives in to Elizabeth's wishes and those of his father, marries her, and sees her dead at the Monster's hands. Elizabeth, as a female victim of the sentimental myth, has the power only to tame or feminize Victor. She has not been able to do so before their marriage (as far as she knows, although it is her feminizing influence in part that has brought him to the creation of the Monster in his successful attempt to perfect his own sentimental masculine character), simply because he has escaped from the domestic circle and thus from her influence. There is no real place in the world for Elizabeth except as Victor's wife, for to go on living with her father she will have to go on living with Victor. Thus she must marry him if she possibly can, and thus she must not object to whatever mysterious actions he takes in connection with the marriage. Waiting in her bridal suite for the Monster to appear, Elizabeth is as helpless, although as self-implicated, a victim as the sentimental/Gothic myth can create.

The first two victims of the Monster, William and indirectly Justine Moritz, are likewise victims of the myth at least partly through their own actions. Victor's small brother, as young as he is, has a sentimental image to live up to—that of the romantic child, cherubic and happy but already manly—and a role to play as he attempts to live up to it. Poor William is already sufficiently sentimentalized to hate the Monster on sight, and, when Victor's unhappy creature attempts to make friends with the child in the hope that one so young will not be prejudiced against him, the little boy shrieks and fights, threatening to tell his father to punish the Monster. Thus the creature, learning of the child's connection with his own creator and tormentor, goes into a rage and, without actually intending to kill William, strangles him to death.

Justine, arrested on the false evidence the Monster has left in her clothing (a miniature of Caroline Frankenstein in a locket William wore), is doomed first simply because of her appearance. The Monster, judging her correctly as one of the sentimental females who will always flee from him, takes his revenge by implicating her in murder. Far from attempting to save herself (knowing how damning and at the same time how false the evidence is, Justine might certainly have said she had taken it earlier from William for safekeeping), the girl actually confesses to the crime. Although she will later rescind the confession, she is still thought guilty—even Elizabeth is not thoroughly convinced of her innocence—and she is sentenced to death. (Elizabeth herself has declared her own guilt for the child's death because she allowed him to wear the miniature, whose theft she supposes to have been the motive for the killing. As Kate Ellis says, "Both Justine and Elizabeth have learned well the lessons of submissiveness...that Caroline...epitomized for them" [133]. More specifically, they both have learned the acceptance of guilt, the "victim mentality" than enables them to cooperate more than passively with the myth that sees them most perfect in death.)

What we know of the characters of all these people—Alphonse and Caroline Frankenstein, Elizabeth, Justine, little William—insofar as they are individuals, Victor reveals almost in spite of himself. They reveal themselves through certain actions that he (or the Monster) describes, but as far as Victor is consciously aware they are all inseparable from the sentimental roles in which they are cast. Likewise, Victor's relationship with each of them is, in his own perception of it, scarcely a real, personal relationship at all, but rather a wooden set of postures taken by role players on the stage of the sentimental convention (for we know that Victor's narrative is a sincere endeavor to communicate a truth to Walton, and that he will distort situations only insomuch as it is in him always to see distortedly). Thus Victor is baffled and dismayed by the tragic outcomes of his relationships, just as he is horrified by—but totally without understanding of—the incestuous and necrophilic dream he experienced following the Monster's vivification, and just as he is horrified and dismayed by the Monster himself. The human complexities that exist within any close relationship—even that between him and his small brother whom he has scarcely known, simply because they are brothers—are not apparent to Victor, partly through his own self-imposed, self-protective blindness, and partly as a result of the successful role playing of the others. Therefore, what happens between Victor and each of them happens to a great extent beneath the level of consciousness, and certainly beneath the level of conscious control, although Victor is somehow aware of his own culpability, much as he is aware of his involvement in the Monster's guilt without being able to control the Monster's behavior.

Victor's relationship with Henry Clerval, too, is governed in what he consciously admits and reveals of it by the terms of the sentimental myth. Clerval is his childhood playfellow, his faithful companion, his "better self"; in other words, he is the romantic and sentimental ideal of a friend, the person for whom Walton longs and Victor grieves. But he is so little characterized as an individual that we do not know what the basis of their friendship may have been, nor do we see Clerval himself revealed as a person by his own actions except in a negative way: his ambitions, whatever they consisted of, have been sublimated (according to Victor) by the feminine influence of Elizabeth even during their childhood. His hopes of attending the university along with Victor, however strong they may have been, are thwarted by his father's wishes that he remain in the family trade. He convinces his father to allow him to leave only that he might help Victor through a long breakdown following the Monster's creation in Ingolstadt, and he again interrupts his own occupation, whatever that may be, to accompany Victor on the British tour where he will become the Monster's second murder victim. In both of these last instances, he is acting on Elizabeth's wishes. Perhaps one reason for Clerval's being especially susceptible to the feminine influence is his childhood reading in "books of chivalry and romance" (37), from which he may have derived an attraction to the idea of courtly love.

On the tour of England and Scotland, Clerval responds both to the scenic beauties and the human companionship he and Victor encounter with a liveliness and sensibility that Victor is no longer able to muster, but that he looks upon as "the image of my former self" (158), the ideal to which he cannot conform. It is significant that Victor sees his friend as an image of himself. Clerval is indeed—at least partly by his own acquiescence—a doppelgänger for Victor, as Victor describes him to Walton: "we are unfashioned creatures, but half made up, if one wiser, better, dearer than ourselves—such a friend ought to be—do not lend his aid to perfectionate our own weak and faulty natures. I once had a friend . . . " (28–29). So Victor first speaks of Clerval, in terms that seem almost those a sentimental lover might use to describe his beloved. They are appropriate terms, for Clerval has been taught by Elizabeth to make "doing good the end and aim of his soaring ambition." Ironically, though Victor describes Clerval as his better half, the friend to "perfectionate

[his] faulty nature," this friend, in his essentially depleted role, is able to do nothing to save Victor from his fate; his death indeed is part of Victor's fate. As with Elizabeth herself, the feminine influence is powerless at last against the excessive masculinity of the Monster.

Victor uses his sentimentalized friendship for Clerval, like his sentimentalized love for Elizabeth, as a substitute for the human passions to which he may not own. The British tour, which Victor describes at length, is one long procrastination during which Victor attempts to avoid the real purpose of his journey. To substitute a sightseeing tour with a male friend for the creation of a female monster is Victor's last sad hope; the very length at which he describes it (another of the supposed flaws in the novel's construction) demonstrates how desperately he wishes not to arrive at its end.

Even when the Monster is seen as having objective existence, Victor is in one sense at least, the sense in which he intends his admission of guilt to the authorities who arrested him, responsible for Clerval's death and for the deaths of William, Justine, Elizabeth, and his father as well. In fact, he is responsible for the suffering of everyone connected with him, because the Monster he deliberately created and continues to reject is the cause of that suffering. He is tragic, in part, because he is responsible. At the same time, Victor is himself a victim of the world he inhabits. It is his tragedy to suffer through the pain and death of those he loves, to suffer the isolation of which their deaths are both the sign and the culmination, for the sentimental world has isolated him from them all his life. His fate is visited upon him because of the nature of his world and because of his own nature as a hero in and of that world.

As W. H. Auden writes, "The tragic situation . . . is not created by the flaw in the hero's character, but is sent to him by the gods as a punishment for having such a flaw" (1). Auden is referring here to the hero of Greek tragedy—specifically of Oedipus—and his thesis contrasts that figure with the hero of Christian tragedy, who, says Auden, is visited by misfortune not as punishment but as "a temptation to sin, an opportunity to choose." Victor must be seen as the first type, the classic hero; at no point does his misfortune present him with an opportunity for choice, but rather it becomes increasingly clear that he has had no real choice. His hubris (the presumption shown in his creating and rejecting the Monster) is thrust upon him by the sentimental culture, which despite its pietistic trappings is essentially a non-Christian (as Auden would define Christian) world view. Victor suffers more than his fellows—more, for instance, than Clerval—because he has responded more heroically to the sentimental world view than they. Furthermore, he has some true understanding of his own guilt, and, given the nature of the Monster, of the inevitability of his guilt, although his understanding is necessarily incomplete.

Victor's relationships—troubled, distorted, misapprehended, and finally shattered as they all are—are indeed the punishment visited upon him for his flaw, which is his ironically Promethean pride. "Generous and self-devoted being!" the Monster calls him at the end (219). The paradoxical truth of this description may be grasped when we recognize that Victor's attempt to assert his sentimental masculinity and at the same time to rid himself of it, his simultaneous creation and rejection of the Monster, is at once a successful effort to be what his sentimental culture demands of him and a disastrous act of self-alienation. To fulfill his role as a sentimental hero—the incomplete masculine ideal whose highest good is domestic affection—he must also fulfill the opposite but inescapable consequence of that role, becoming the *isolato,* the stranger, the guilt-ridden creator of the Monster who reduces his domestic circle to carnage. The hero of sentiment cannot escape his Gothic shadow.

There is one more element to be considered if we would understand Frankenstein as a tragic figure, and in considering it we are led back to the novel's concentric structure. This element is the character of the Monster; to find who and what the Monster is, and what his place is in Victor Frankenstein's tragedy, we must first contrast him with Victor, and then go beyond his own central story and Victor's encompassing narrative into the Walton narrative, the frame that encircles the other two and leads directly to Mrs. Seville, to the world outside the Frankenstein story, and to us, the readers of the novel.

As a hero of the sentimental myth, Victor Frankenstein is necessarily incomplete. As he presents himself in his own narrative, he seems curiously flat, two-dimensional, lacking those human qualities—including even the capacity for great suffering, although he says he suffers—that a truly tragic hero ought to possess. Like the other characters of whom he speaks in his narrative, he becomes real only when he reveals himself through some of the actions he reports—for example, his behavior in Justine's prison cell, when he and Elizabeth visit the condemned young woman and Victor cannot bring himself to speak to her. Here, as in the incidents surrounding Elizabeth's death, including Victor's wild prowling of the halls in search of the Monster, his hysterical reaction to the sight of Elizabeth's corpse, and his pursuit of the murderer that he alone has seen, the mask of sentimental masculinity that he has taken for his own identity slips, and we see the real person that Victor has become—weak, ineffectual, but at least human.

In these glimpses we gain a degree of sympathy for Victor, and we may recognize a certain heroism in the brave effort he makes to resume the mask, to be what his code demands of him. Ironically, it is only in these revelations of what Victor himself considers unmanly weakness that he becomes an attractive character. In his doomed, even absurd (as when, on the brink of death from exposure, he inquires about Walton's destination before he will board the explorer's ship) determination to enact his sentimental role, he emerges as greater than that role.

We feel this—both the incompleteness and the heroic effort to stand in spite of it—about Victor when Walton first describes him as a man who "must have been a noble creature in his better days, being even now in wreck so attractive and amiable" (27). Nor has it been the last, torturous pursuit of the Monster, nor the step-by-step destruction of his domestic world, that has reduced him to this wreck, for we learn from his own narrative that, except for a deceptive period of recovery (which is also one of "almost insupportable sensitiveness" [68]) just before receiving news of William's death, Victor has been depleted, a "wreck" of himself, ever since the Monster's awakening. Indeed, because he tells his own story only a short while before his death, Victor never appears to Walton directly, or to us, in any but the curiously depleted state in which the creation of the Monster leaves him.

Moreover, in Victor's account of his life up to that moment—the romantically idealized childhood, the purportedly blissful school days—we see little more than the same self-imposed mask. Even then, it seems, sentimental role playing substituted, at least in retrospect, for human identity. Even in Victor's description of his emotions at the death of his mother, he seems rather to be striking a pose or painting a picture (like the portrait of Caroline at her father's coffin) than to be reporting real, human behavior, although the posture may be imposed after the fact at the suggestion of a faulty, sentimentally influenced memory.

The only real difference between the pre-Monster and post-Monster Victors is that the real Victor, glimpsed in moments of self-revelation occurring throughout the narrative, is noticeably more energetic before the Monster's appearance. Whereas he has become enervated, incapable of decisive action or strong feeling after the Monster's creation, he was apparently determined, curious, and passionate before that event. There is a ring of truth to his descriptions of his intellectual curiosity that is lacking in those other passages in which he recalls his childhood and adolescent emotions. Significantly, Victor has interpreted as "intellectual" his strongest consciously held emotions, and has invested all of his genuine emotion, thus misidentified, in his passionate pursuit of scientific knowledge. Therefore, when the pursuit culminates in the Monster's creation, and when Victor retreats in horror from his creature, his emotional energy, inadmissible in any other area of his life (where he has substituted sentimental sensibility for real emotion), is drained from him. However—and this is perhaps the central truth of Mary Shelley's novel—the emotional energy Victor has lost does not simply dissipate; it is transferred, out of Victor's control, to the Monster.

With the loss of his emotional energy, all invested in the single-minded pursuit of science, and then drained into the Monster (whom Victor calls "my own vampire, my own spirit let loose from the grave, and forced to destroy all that was dear to me" [77]), Victor loses his power to realize the full depth of his tragic experience. By his dying words ("Farewell, Walton! Seek happiness in tranquillity, and avoid ambition. . . . Yet why do I say this? I have myself been blasted in these hopes, yet another may succeed" [217–18]), Victor reveals that, although he recognizes his own guilt, he does not truly recognize its nature nor the hopelessness of any success that another, like himself, may attain. Full recognition of the tragedy, like a full range of human emotions, is reserved for his creature, the Monster, who is as much a protagonist of the tragedy as Victor himself, and who is invested with all those human qualities that Victor, as the "perfectionated" sentimental hero, has denied in his own character.

Part of the Monster's tragic recognition is indeed contained within the Frankenstein narrative, as the central section recalled and related by Victor in the Monster's words. As we have seen, the Monster's story is in great part a parable intended by its teller to teach Victor about the nature of the sentimental myth, its contradictions and flaws, and his own participation in it—including his relationship to the being he has created and rejected. If only to the extent that Victor recalls the Monster's narrative and reports it, he understands that narrative; and his understanding becomes more complex if we consider the Monster to be in any psychological sense Victor's doppelgänger.

Still, Victor's understanding stops short of true recognition because of his intractable alienation from his creature. In fact, his refusal to accept the Monster is precisely a refusal to recognize and accept the truth of what the Monster's narrative means. And inevitably Victor's refusal to recognize and accept the Monster is what prevents him from regaining his own emotional energy and from establishing real relationships with his family and friends. The fact that, to be true in his own mind to them and to himself, he *must* refuse and reject the Monster makes his rejection no less deliberate. Like all tragic heroes, Victor behaves paradoxically in that his heroism and his transgression are one and the same act. Unlike any other tragic hero, Victor has (really or symbolically, and the novel allows for *both* possibilities) divided himself so radically by his heroic and transgressive act that he shares his heroism and his tragedy with his creature, who is also his double.

The Monster has revealed himself, in his central narrative, to be more emotionally aware, more human, than his creator. Compare both characters' statements on the natural world, for example:

[Victor:] When happy, inanimate nature had the power of bestowing on me the most delightful sensations. A serene sky and verdant fields filled me with ecstasy. The present season was indeed divine; the flowers of spring blossomed in the hedges, while those of summer were already in bud. I was undisturbed by thoughts. . . . (70)

[The Monster:] Several changes of day and night passed, and the orb of night had greatly lessened, when I began to distinguish my sensations from each other. I gradually saw plainly the clear stream that supplied me with drink, and the trees that shaded me with their foliage. I was delighted when I first discovered that a pleasant sound, which often saluted my ears, proceeded from the throats of the little winged animals which had often intercepted the light from my eyes. (103)

or on human affection:

[Victor:] [Elizabeth's] sympathy was [mine and Clerval's]; her smile, her soft voice, the sweet glance of her celestial eyes, were ever there to bless and animate us. She was the living spirit of love to soften and attract; I might have become sullen in my study, rough through the ardour of my nature, but that she was there to subdue me to a semblance of her own gentleness. And Clerval—could aught ill entrench on the noble spirit of Clerval?—yet he might not have been so perfectly humane . . . had she not unfolded to him the real loveliness of beneficence. . . . (38)

[The Monster:] I could mention innumerable instances which, although slight, marked the disposition of these amiable cottagers. In the midst of poverty and want, Felix carried with pleasure to his sister the first little white flower that peeped out from beneath the snowy ground. Early in the morning, before she had risen, he cleared away the snow that obstructed her path to the milk-house, drew water from the well, and brought the wood . . . [that the Monster had secretly gathered and stacked] from the out-house. . . . [Then,] as there was little to do in the frosty season, he read to the old man and Agatha. (113)

I formed in my imagination a thousand pictures of presenting myself to them, and their reception of me. I imagined that they would be disgusted until, by my gentle demeanor and conciliating words, I should first win their favour, and afterward their love. (115)

Even allowing for the Monster's inexperience with the world into which he has been "born" and rudely ejected as a full-grown being without friend or direction, still his descriptions, not only of the objective phenomena he observes but also of his subjective reaction to them, are noticeably less stilted, less trite, more apparently sincere than are Victor's. While he and Victor both use a fairly ornate sentence style and vocabulary, the Monster's descriptions are simpler and more direct in both respects. His reference to specific, concrete detail contrasts especially strikingly with Victor's vague generalizations. It is apparent throughout his imbedded narrative that the Monster is more emotionally alive, more willing to recognize his own vulnerability, and thus more open, than his creator.

Unfortunately, the Monster's emotional directness is not limited to the positive feelings of wonder, affection, and joy; he also feels unhappiness and rage, and his passions, like those of a child, are violent. But at least until Victor's destruction of the female monster, the creature's violence is not really malicious even when he encounters and recognizes what he perceives as malice directed against him. The killing of young William, like the destruction of the deserted DeLacey cottage, is prompted by frustration and rage and is hardly a premeditated act. The violence that the Monster perpetrates is his understandable reaction to the treatment he has received from everyone, including Victor, from the moment of his awakening—and even before, since his hideousness is Victor's handiwork.

There is a clue to the nature of his destructiveness in Victor's remark that the Monster is "forced to destroy" (77) what Victor loves. The force that drives the Monster to violence is both positive and negative. He is driven by the passionate emotions and hostilities Victor cannot acknowledge as his own, but his passions are beyond his control: Victor, whose essence is self-control, refuses to be his creature's master, and the creature cannot be his own. But, although the Monster is thus as fated as Victor to enact a tragic role, his plea to Victor for control reveals that he sees, more surely than does Victor, the nature of his fate. He is more capable of tragic recognition, of true humanity, than his creator. To learn the depth of the Monster's humanity, we must go to the outer circle of narrative, the Walton frame.

Walton's narrative is important for a number of reasons. First, it establishes a protagonist who is not incomplete, as both Victor and the Monster are. Walton is divided, in his mutually exclusive goals of discovery and affection which, since he sees them in the same light as Victor has seen his goals, will lead if he pursues them to the sentimental masculine ideal, bringing with it a fatal alienation from his own humanity and thus from all possibility of real domestic affection or unflawed creative endeavor. But Walton has, before Victor's death, turned back in his voyage toward this divided end; he is still capable of resolving the difference between his ambition and his need for affection. He *may* heal the division within himself and become heroic beyond the terms of sentimentality—although as the novel ends he has not yet done so.

Second, Walton's narrative is important because it links the other two narratives together within itself. By Walton's direct encounters with both Victor and the Monster, his narrative brings all of the levels of the novel to its own realistic level; if either Victor or the Monster is in any sense unreal, or if they both are (for example, if they are figures in Walton's unconscious brought to consciousness in the form of a dream to warn him of the psychic and actual danger he is in), Walton at least believes them to be real, to share equally in his own reality, which is all we can demand of any novel's narrator. Walton, insofar as he is demonstrably sane, gives us a perspective on Victor's degree of sanity; if the Monster is an aspect of Victor's personality, then the creature's identity, outliving the creator's, must be sufficiently strong to convince Walton that he is actually seeing (for a moment—he shuts his eyes almost immediately) and conversing with another individual after Victor's death. (The absence of detail about the disposal of Victor's body, after the

Monster's disappearance into "darkness and distance," although such detail would admittedly weaken the ending of the novel, may lend some support to this view; Walton may be present at Victor's "death" as Victor—and may later see him, as the Monster, leave the ship.)

Third, Walton's narrative gives us the opportunity to encounter the Monster's point of view, his identity as an equal participant in Victor's tragedy, without Victor's interference. After Victor's death, the creature appears in Walton's ship's cabin, where the explorer discovers him "utter[ing] exclamations of grief and horror" (218). In the Monster's subsequent statements, with which the book ends, we find the full revelation of the Monster's character and of the tragedy that he and Victor share.

The Monster's final statements confirm his emotional depth and his superiority to Victor in this regard. Obviously grief-stricken at Victor's death, he tells Walton of how he suffered as a result of his own actions in destroying Victor's world:

> A frightful selfishness hurried me on, while my heart was poisoned with remorse. Think you that the groans of Clerval were music to my ears? My heart was fashioned to be susceptible of love and sympathy; and, when wrenched by misery to vice and hatred, it did not endure the violence of the change, without torture such as you cannot even imagine. (219–20)

When Walton, with apparent justification, accuses him of hypocrisy, the Monster denies the accusation, but says that he expects no sympathy and that he is "satisfied that abhorrence and opprobrium" should be given him after his death (221). He continues, "Once I falsely hoped to meet with beings, who, pardoning my outward form, would love me for the excellent qualities which I was capable of unfolding. . . . But now crime has degraded me . . . the fallen angel becomes a malignant devil" (221). And, justly, the Monster points out that he has not been "the only criminal": "Why do you not hate Felix, who drove his friend from his door with contumely? Why do you not execrate the rustic, who sought to destroy the savior of his child?" (221–22). Why, he might as well go on, is Agatha or Safie, Elizabeth or Justine, even little William, not to be blamed for looking no further than the outward form and fearing the creature who inhabited it?—except that, as with Victor, whom the Monster does not accuse, the violence these others turned against him was not physical, but only the emotional violence of rejection and repulsion. Even Walton, to listen to the Monster, must shut his eyes.

The Monster, in claiming his sufferings to be greater than Victor's, is *not* making a hypocritical plea for pity; he is indeed the greater sufferer, if only because he has more human capacity for suffering, as he has more human capacity for all feelings. But he suffers more tragically, as well, because he is not only conscious of the wrongs done him but also aware of his own guilt and of its nature. The "frightful selfishness" that drove him to his crimes is indeed the Monster's flaw, but it is his greatness as well, in the sense that his selfishness is nothing more or less than his passionate awareness of life, of his own individuality, and his drive—stemming from that awareness—to love and cherish his fellow beings. This is the awareness that Victor stifled in himself, the drive that he feared, the powerful and essentially erotic (thus potentially dangerous) passion that he banished from himself in creating the Monster. In the creature, the force became not only uncontrollable (for only Victor might have controlled it, and he refused to do so), but also perverted, for to the sentimental myth the power of *eros* is intrinsically fearful and ugly, intrinsically linked with all dark and inadmissible emotions, and is thus deprived of creative, loving outlets and forced into channels of violence and destruction. The Monster, tragically, sees his own nature, and knows that the very remorse it imposes upon him is "poisonous" to his heart, which is rejected by those it would love because of what it is, and which still cannot stop being what it is.

It is Victor's tragedy to be closed, loveless, unaware of his selfishness (really, of his *self*), and only partly aware of his responsibility for what has happened; it is the Monster's to be completely aware of the reasons for his suffering, including his own actions, and still unable to change either the causes of that suffering or his awareness of it. It is the tragedy of both—and perhaps the tragedy of the sentimental/Gothic myth—that the only salvation for either Victor or the Monster lies in their reconciliation, while the nature of each, in its own way, makes their reconciliation absolutely impossible.

3

The Myth's Survival:
Monsters in Our Time

Any myth becomes a source of metaphor; myth is itself a metaphor, a human way of ordering the otherwise chaotic experience of reality into some apparently meaningful pattern that can be comprehended, if not fully understood, in human terms. Thus in a sense every human being possesses his or her own mythos, his or her own way of making sense of the universe, each a variation upon the dominant mythos of that individual's culture—in most cases, no doubt, a very slight variation, but in others a greater one. For example, to use an illustration cited earlier, the individual mythos of Sigmund Freud, developed from and certainly partaking of the dominant cultural mythos of his time (and also of those other views of reality that Freud's experience and education afforded him), became a variation of his culture's world view significant enough that it changed that world view in striking ways.

The sentimental/Gothic myth, dominant in Western culture for so many years, provided a rich source of metaphor for the perceiving and ordering of experience. That mythos has produced enormously significant effects on the actual shape of experience, the nature of the world it helped to create, for a variety of reasons related to the nature of the myth itself. Because of its roots in middle-class, patriarchal, capitalistic enterprise, it has helped to assure the almost unprecedented success of that enterprise within little more than two and a half centuries. And because of its self-divided nature, the myth has made it not only possible but necessary for the conscious, controlling element of that enterprise to view its own nature, its motives, and its success in a characteristically shortsighted, one-sided way, disguising to itself its complete and actual nature, refusing to admit the close relationship between its nature and its often horrific consequences, revealing to itself its Gothic completion only in dark dreams and cautionary tales.

Virgin Land: The Frontier Myth and Its Monsters

To see how the sentimental/Gothic myth has worked in only one area of experience, let us examine, necessarily briefly, several facets of the relationship between human beings and the land on the North American continent, and how that relationship has been reflected in mythic tradition.

The relationship is based upon a metaphoric premise common to mythologies far more ancient than the sentimental/Gothic myth (and attested by such writers as Sir James Frazer in *The Golden Bough,* Joseph Campbell in *The Masks of God,* and Robert Graves in *The White Goddess,* on whose scholarship my argument draws). This premise, simply stated, is that the earth is female. This analogy was obviously attractive even for nonagrarian cultures who saw similarities between the bearing of young and the bearing of fruit, between the cycle of seasons and the female cycles of estrus and fertility, and its strength can only have become more apparent with the development of agriculture and experience in the breeding of domestic animals. Thus in many ancient mythologies the earth was depicted as female, and rituals associated with gathering, or with planting, irrigation, and harvesting, evolved to ensure the earth's fertility, often involving human sexual behavior used as sympathetic magic.

Not surprisingly, fertility rites based on this ancient premise survived into medieval and even later times, often incorporated into Christian celebrations, in British and European agricultural communities. Thus it is scarcely remarkable that, within the sentimental/Gothic myth, the land should have remained somehow feminine and that the products of the land—not merely agricultural but also of forestry, mining, fishing—should have continued to be seen as somehow analogous to the products of female fertility.

It may be noted, however, that much of the older mythic material regarding the land as female contains elements foreign to the sentimental/Gothic myth. In many of the older traditions, for example, the female persona of the earth is matched with one or more male personae representing other elements such as sky, sun, rain. The fertility of the earth may be seen as partly a function of the male element or elements, so that human activity is important as a means of persuading these metaphoric persons to perform their characteristic roles. Rituals may be performed in direct connection with or apart from actual agricultural activities, gathering, or hunting, but the persuasive rite itself is an acknowledgment and propitiation of the power held by the earth and the related elements. Furthermore, as evidence from both agricultural and hunting and gathering cultures suggests, the products of the earth's fertility are often regarded as important entities in their own right, requiring propitiation and respect from the human beings who use them. Thus a characteristic attitude reflected in many older mythic traditions is that power resides in the earth and related elements—in nature as distinct from human nature—and that those human beings who are most successful in making use of the elements are those who are most skilled at propitiating them, persuading them to be generous and fruitful. Almost always, human activities and roles seem to be part of a system of sympathetic magic invoking the power involved in nature, rather than as actual human power interacting with or acting directly upon the passive potential of nature.

Within the sentimental/Gothic myth, however, the relationship of humanity—*mankind*—to the feminine earth is precisely that of masculinity to femininity throughout the myth. It is on one level a conscious, idealized, prescribed relationship in which the masculine element, mankind, is supposed to use the active power central to its role to protect, support, control, and fertilize the passive, feminine element, nature (the land and related elements, including the land's products); in return mankind expects domestic comforts, fruitfulness, and material profit. On a deeper, unconscious level, the relationship is one of hostility, exploitation, and violence; nature by its very passivity seems to resist mankind's efforts to subdue and shape it. It is maddeningly enigmatic, it threatens to domesticate man, and the more he ravages it the weaker and less resilient it becomes—so that he resorts to more and more violent means and implements, more and more monstrous images of himself, in an irrational and finally uncontrollable fury of vengeance directed both at the land and at the kindly husbandman he had willed and imagined himself to be. In effect, mankind becomes divided, destroying the earth he professes to love and at the same time standing helplessly by, unable to control the forces he himself has set in motion.

The sentimental/Gothic myth has been told and retold in American frontier novels and romances for nearly two centuries; many of these tales, like many of the other traditional manifestations of the myth, are stock, formulaic expressions, pulp and paperback westerns and low-budget films destined to be consumed and forgotten. A few, either by virtue of unusual artistry or because of antisentimental elements that recommend them to a critical audience trained to appreciate twentieth-century literary realism, are widely enough known to provide effective examples of the myth's transference to a frontier setting. One such work, Jack Schaefer's 1949 novel *Shane,* recently reissued in a popular edition but perhaps best known from the 1952 Paramount film directed by George Stevens, illustrates succinctly the ways in which the mythic material is manifested in this setting. Although the film follows Schaefer's novel in substance, the A. B. Guthrie screenplay differs from the book in a number of significant particulars. Moreover, the film's visual element allows much of the mythic material to appear directly, without verbal presentation; thus, my discussion will be of the film rather than the novel.

Shane, like other sentimental expressions, presents domesticity as the ideal state; the perfect place is the homesteader's house, to which Shane is welcomed as the story opens. Here is the warm heart of the sentimental tradition, with Joe Starrett's family and the families of the other settlers representing the ideal of domestic affection supported by thrift, hard work, and temperance, built on connubial love, and celebrated at a festive gathering of families on the occasion of the Starretts' wedding anniversary (Independence Day, which is jokingly said to mark Joe's loss of independence). The antithesis of the settlers' homes is the local cattle rancher's headquarters—not, as might be expected, at a ranch house, but in the town, a stark, almost surrealistic group of unpainted wooden buildings set in a line against a dramatically jagged mountain range (the western slopes of the Wyoming Tetons appear in the film), where the rancher and his men hold court in a saloon. The rancher's forces, the villains in this sentimental drama, apparently are without wives and families—indeed, there are few women in evidence in the town—but their saloon is separated only by a set of swinging half-doors from the general store in which the settlers' families gather to shop and gossip. The cattlemen, who have been awarded a government contract to sell beef to an Indian reservation, are engaged in an effort to drive the homesteaders—"squatters" as the cattlemen call them—off the land that both sides claim: one as range, the other as farmland. We never see any of the ranch hands working; instead, they spend their nights and days plotting against the settlers, intimidating them, driving cattle herds across their gardens and fields, and setting fire to their homes.

The characters in *Shane* are typically sentimental/Gothic figures. Joe Starrett is a perfect sentimental hero inasmuch as he has been tamed and rid of his excessive masculinity (he is glad to have lost his independence), and although he valiantly stands up to the evil opposition, he is essentially helpless against his foes. Indeed, when the ranchers hire Jack Wilson to run the settlers off their land, Starrett can scarcely persuade his fellow homesteaders to stay. Their masculinity, like that of Jonathan Harker, has been depleted by the proximity of the Gothic figure who has come into play against them. Joe's wife, Marian, is likewise a perfect sentimental figure, the good wife and mother whose femininity has domesticized her husband and who, though more conventionally attractive than the other settlers' wives, is depicted as being almost without sexual qualities.

Shane, the central figure whose mythic proportions are especially evident to the point-of-view character—Starrett's preadolescent son, called Bob in the novel but Joey in the film—is a hero of the Byronic type. He is excessively masculine but for that very reason attractive to the sentimental characters, and apparently capable of being domesticized—although ambiguously so, for when the film ends we are not sure whether he has refused the sentimental tempering of his character or has recognized the impossibility of its being accomplished.

Shane embodies the masculine characteristics most valued by the myth—bravery, honesty, strength, vitality—but there are also suggestions that he may be the mythic outlaw, temporarily disguising himself for the sake of the settlers because he is attracted to the domesticity they represent. He is also attracted to Marian, as she is to him, and the possibility of his domestication through their mutual love is implied; but since Marian is already Joe's wife there is no place in the domestic circle for Shane. (A frequent variation of this situation in other novels and films has the female character married either to an excessively masculine or a completely depleted man, whose death allows the attraction between her and the Byronic hero to develop into the typical sentimental courtship drama.) It is Shane's excessive masculinity that permits him to help Starrett and the other settlers after he has decided to adopt the pose of domestication, a decision symbolized by his donning of work clothes similar to Starrett's.

At Shane's first appearance, Starrett recognizes him as a potential threat to his sentimental domestic ideal, but, when the newcomer takes his side against the ranchers, Starrett is urged by Marian to invite him into their home. Later, after Shane has decided to stay for a time with the Starretts, he and Joe go into town, and when Shane appears in the saloon he is *not* recognized as an "outlaw" by the enemy; in Starrett's company, he seems to the cattlemen to be one of the feminine-influenced settlers, and his acceptance of the ranch-hand Chris's insult signals his willingness to assume this disguise. In the sequel to this scene, with the settlers and their wives in the store, Shane again enters the saloon, is taunted by Chris, and reveals his true masculine identity by knocking his antagonist into the feminine area on the other side of the swinging saloon doors. The rancher (named Fletcher in the novel but Rufe Ryker in the film) then tries to win the newcomer over to his side, but Shane refuses; the fight that ensues pits Shane against the entire mob of villains, but he is joined by Starrett and together they defeat the opposition. It is at this point that Ryker summons the Gothic gunfighter, Jack Wilson, to combat not the settlers but the other excessively masculine figure who has aligned himself with them, and whose true nature is now apparent.

Wilson, the soft-spoken hired killer, is as much a Gothic monster as Frankenstein's creature or Dracula. Black-hatted and black-vested, possessed of a wild vitality within an aura of deadly stillness, he is swift to answer Ryker's summons, but he has no interest in the rancher's plans or motives and apparently little interest in his fee; what interests him is death. That is his business, his purpose. He must be persuaded not to gun down two of the settlers as they ride through town; he is eager to do what he does best. Even the rancher and his crew are half afraid of him—as the settlers are of Shane—because they recognize in him the outlaw who threatens even their form of outlawry, the madness and wildness that they occasionally toy with but have rejected for the sake of civilization. (In other versions of the myth, the hired gunfighter, having accomplished his assigned murders, is in turn murdered by his employers or murders them in turn; like all Gothic monsters he depends on civilization for his existence but paradoxically cannot coexist with civilized humanity, for he embodies every element that civilized humanity rejects: lawlessness, violence, the intense passion that is satisfied not by love or creation but by death.)

Wilson (Stark Wilson in Schaefer's novel but Jack Wilson in the film) is, as his name suggests, a dark double for Shane; both are lone, mysterious wanderers, both drawn into the settler-rancher conflict apparently by the participants but both finally rejecting the participants' motives even as they draw the conflict into their own beings and settle it between themselves. As they face each other in the film, Wilson is the dark shadow of Shane, the shadow that has pursued him into the sentimental heart of the settlers' valley; he is what Shane might be, what he may still be, and the decisive gunfight is a victory for the sentimental forces only because, after killing Wilson, Shane rides away. In a sense, he is taking the Gothic shadow with him, having become again what he was before, what Wilson was. A man must be what he is, he tells the boy. But before leaving, Shane has beaten Starrett, draining the farmer of the excessive masculine vitality that his earlier presence had lent him. And before leaving, he has instilled some of his own outlawry, a spark of Gothic darkness, into Starrett's son. Although the valley is now truly the perfect sentimental place, without guns and gunfighters, it may not always remain so.

Shane is obviously in some ways a retelling of the sentimental/Gothic myth in Western guise, and as such it is decidedly more sentimental than Gothic, for sentimental values are upheld throughout; there is no real doubt throughout the film that Ryker at least will be defeated, though Shane is, interestingly, nearly enough a potential Christ-figure that Wilson's triumph over him is dramatically possible. (The emphatic blondness of Alan Ladd in the film, as opposed to the dark Shane of Schaefer's novel, and his identification with Joey, the son of Joseph and Marian, suggest this; however, the emergence of a Byronic hero as a Christlike character—for example, Christy Mahon in Synge's *Playboy of the Western World*—is not unknown.) But if the central drama of the sentimental/Gothic myth is the courtship of a feminine woman by a masculine man, or her pursuit by a Gothic villain, then *Shane* and similar frontier stories seem to deviate considerably.

However, if it is seen that the passive feminine role in works like these is only peripherally filled by the female characters, that the central feminine figure is the land itself, then not only is the courtship/pursuit theme reinstated but also the apparently sentimental outcome of the work is rendered considerably more ambiguous.

There is a good deal of evidence that the land, in this case the disputed valley, is a central figure in *Shane*. The rather fulsome descriptions of the valley's beauty employed in Schaefer's novel give way, in the film, to the more effective device of photography; the film is all but dominated by the romantic, pictorial splendor of the valley itself, the mountains, the sky. It is apparent, too, that Starrett is courting the land and means to win it. On the first evening of Shane's visit, Starrett tells the newcomer that he *loves* his homestead, that he will not leave it while he lives. When he attempts to persuade the other settlers to stay in the valley, rather than stressing the difficulty of resettling elsewhere he appeals to their devotion to this particular place. When their wives and his own wife wish to leave, Starrett insists upon staying, again appealing to the men's love of the valley. It is, as he sees it, a *good* valley, beautiful, meant to raise crops and farm animals; Starrett is in effect rescuing the valley from Ryker, who will allow his cattle to overrun and overgraze it, who has himself only a proprietory interest in mastering the land and taking all he can from it, having in his own words tamed it—that is, wrested it away from the Indians who had hunted there years before.

Starrett's relationship to the land is like that of the sentimental suitor to his beloved: he is attracted by its beauty, drawn by its fertility, willing to sacrifice his own independence to stay with it permanently. (Ryker in desperation offers him a job, but Starrett refuses.) The land will yield itself to him and will at the same time tame him, for as a farmer he will be governed by its seasons and its whims. Ryker, on the other hand, means to take what he can from the valley and move on. He has no home there; he is presented as an opportunist, a seducer who wants conquest without commitment. He is jealous beyond reason of the settlers' claims—but perhaps not beyond reason after all, for he knows that when they have "won" the valley he will not be able to abuse it further, and knows too that their dependence upon the land is an insult to his jealously guarded independence.

What is the relationship between Shane or Wilson and the land? At first glance, apparently none; they are both wanderers, traditionally men without land, of obscure origins. But as outlaws, in a deeper sense they *own* the land. It is theirs until civilization, even Ryker's limited sort, takes it from them. Shane says that Ryker has lived too long; the days of his open range are over. "What about you, gunfighter?" is Ryker's retort. Shane and Wilson are vestiges of an older kind of outlaw, the "mountain man," the *isolato* related to the land exactly as Melmoth is related to the innocent souls on whom he preys, as Dracula is related to his victims; it is a relationship both intense and impersonal. We see it surface not with Wilson, the known monster, but with Shane, the monster in disguise—first, when he provides the strength Starrett has needed to tear a huge tree stump from his yard, forcing the land to yield to him completely; and finally when Shane rides away from town into the mountains, the country that has not yet been made to yield its splendid but passive innocence to any man but him and his like.

In other American fiction, from *The Grapes of Wrath* and *The Great Gatsby,* in which we see the ravaged wasteland separately from the men or monsters who have reduced it to ruin (though their descendents may continue to ravage it), to Stephen King's long Gothic, *The Stand,* in which plague survivors, followers of the black-suited, not-quite-human Walking Dude, attempt to destroy what is left of the country with nuclear weapons scavenged from abandoned arsenals, we see the Gothic relationship of mankind to the land clearly revealed. But even in such apparently sentimental manifestations as *Shane,* the Gothic direction of mankind's apparently loving attention to the earth becomes plain. Although the sentimental hero is not conscious—cannot allow himself to be conscious—of his own intentions toward the land, he will create and invite monsters, distorted images of himself from gunfighters to giant strip-mining machines, to subdue it for him. Caught in mythic self-division, he may believe his professions of love for the living earth, but at the same time he watches in apparent helplessness and horror as his own chemicals and machines and weapons destroy it; it is most pleasing to him when it submits, even until it is dead.

Like Victor Frankenstein, the doomed sentimental hero, the American frontier hero can gain his mythic self-identity only by denying those elements in himself that he despises and fears, elements that seem to him unmanly or dangerously violent. These traits he projects onto his mythic monsters, outlaws, "squaw-men," and especially the Native Americans whom he has displaced; those characteristics commonly ascribed by popular eighteenth- and nineteenth-century American literature to the American Indian—a paradoxical mixture of demonic hostility, cowardice, and childlike nobility— are precisely those traits that Victor Frankenstein saw in his Monster. Ironically, the violence that the American hero of frontier myth denies in himself has remained, like the rejected Monster, active and destructive but beyond his conscious control. And just as ironically, the unmanly elements (actually, in mythic terms, feminine elements) he has rejected are those very human traits that would allow him to achieve unity with the land.

The Sentimental Tradition: Popular Romances

For much of the nineteenth and early twentieth centuries, western stories, novels, and romances were arguably the most popular genre of popular American literature, challenged only, perhaps, by the love story romance with its historical, "gothic," and other permutations, published for an almost exclusively female audience. Both genres have remained for the most part a kind of subliterature, largely appearing in pulp periodicals (or their contemporary equivalents) and inexpensive books, widely read, but beneath the notice of literary criticism and seldom attaining the distinction of more than one edition—although each type has produced an occasional classic, like Schaefer's *Shane* or the British writer Mary Stewart's *Nine Coaches Waiting,* one of the prototypes of the contemporary "gothic romance." Both types still flourish, their printed forms supplemented by television westerns, soap operas, and miniseries.

The patterns of situation, characterization, and plot in both of these popular genres are inevitably grounded in the terms of the sentimental/Gothic myth; they are generally almost purely sentimental manifestations, although since the early 1970s there has been a resurgence of Gothic literature in the form of horror stories and novels, best exemplified by the work of the prolific writer Stephen King. Any random sampling from the western or romance sections of a paperback book rack will reveal the familiar sentimental conventions: the insistence on middle-class values and virtues, the strong separation of masculine and feminine roles, the central concern with courtship and its complications, and the assurance, through setting and detail, that real life is being portrayed.

Karen Rowe argues that popular romances, which she sees as extensions of the traditional fairy tale, delude readers rather than reinforce cultural models of behavior, since actual social practice is no longer reflected in these idealized mythic expressions. In fact, despite the growing divergence between these popular forms and serious—that is, critically accepted—literature, the separation of life and art that Rowe sees may not be as great or as significant as it appears.

Throughout the period of the sentimental tradition, some degree of separation has been acknowledged. Much of the irony of Jane Austen's novels, for example, takes its edge from the reader's awareness of the difference between the heroine's situation and her own sentimental perception of it, a perception generally colored by her indulgence in popular literature. Still, even Austen's work reveals the extent to which sentimental literature *is* an accurate reflection of and shaping influence upon the world in which its readers exist; the fact that Catherine Moreland in *Northanger Abbey* bases her behavior on her sentimental/Gothic reading, for example, does not make her delusions as apparent to the other characters in the novel as they are to the reader, for she is acting according to social conventions that they observe as well, and even her wild Gothic assumptions only demonstrate the close correspondence between fictional conventions and the real world.

Deluding as the sentimental assurances and role models undoubtedly are, there can be no doubt that they have shaped behavior and expectations and continue to do so, reinforcing themselves as cultural forms. Thus, for example, despite the influence of feminism as a political and social force during various periods in nineteenth- and twentieth-century America, the idea of the traditional woman—that is, the ideal woman of sentimental tradition—is still strong enough to have been a major factor in the post-Vietnam-era opposition to and defeat of the Equal Rights Amendment. And thus, despite the countless exposés of political duplicitousness and corruption, the image of themselves that most male political candidates try to present is that of the strong, honest, forthright family man—in other words, the ideal domesticated man of sentimental literature. It would seem that the existence of the sentimental tradition as a cultural model is still important and somehow comforting.

Moreover, while contemporary popular sentimental literature, from the paperback western to the love story romance, may seem forced to choose in some instances between apparent realism and the traditional sentimental conventions, much of this literature actually does a very good job of reconciling the two. The so-called sexual revolution of the 1960s and 1970s is reflected in the typical romance novel, as is the raised consciousness of the feminist movement, so that the heroine is often portrayed as an economically independent career woman with undisguised sexual feelings, and premarital (even extramarital) sexual relationships are not only acknowledged but often shown as acceptable. Still the conventions remain. True love is the ideal relationship, and it is expected to lead to marriage. The feminine woman may elect to combine marriage and motherhood with her career, but she will certainly not choose the career instead of marriage and motherhood. The masculine man may help out with the housework on occasion, but he and the heroine both understand very well that this is not his normal role. Virtue is rewarded; vice is punished. Plot complications may include anything from conflicting business interests to delayed combat anxiety, but the central conflict is *always* between a Byronic hero who wishes to seduce without losing his freedom and a heroine who wishes to—and eventually does—tame him.

If the sentimental tradition is alive and well in popular late-twentieth-century romance literature, there has, however, been one important difference in the way the sentimental/Gothic myth as a whole has been reflected in the literature of this century. With the emergence of realistic fiction and the subsequently widening gap between popular and serious literature, the Gothic mode apparently disappeared from popular fiction, at least as it had conventionally been represented in the novel from *The Castle of Otranto* to *Dracula*. The reasons for its disappearance are not difficult to trace.

Realism, or a kind of realism, had always been a characteristic of the novel form, and the literature of the sentimental/Gothic myth had always depended upon this apparent realism in the representation of character, setting, and situation to convey the cultural world view it reflected to its audience. Then, with the advent of psychological realism, heavily influenced by radically new social concepts, serious fiction essentially abandoned the romantic views of reality—including the conventional Gothic fantasies—that had dominated English and American literature for over a century. The Gothic strain continued in serious fiction by writers like Henry James, Edith Wharton, and William Faulkner, but as the popular audience came more and more to reject such relatively subtle and difficult fare (and as the audience for a more sophisticated literature grew, allowing established writers to ignore the less sophisticated reader), popular literature tended to follow a few established patterns or formulas, and writers, encouraged by the publishing industry to stay within these formulas, produced what was expected of them. With one very notable exception, there simply was no formula for what had been known as Gothic fiction.

That exception was, of course, one established by a few enterprising editors who saw a popular market for a kind of fantastic, speculative, "weird" fiction still being written by a few nonconformist writers following the tradition—or traditions—of H. G. Wells, Edgar Allan Poe, Jules Verne, Bram Stoker, and Mary Shelley. Growing from other forms of popular adventure fiction, this sort of writing became a kind of synthesis of suspense fiction, ghost stories, grotesque tales, utopian and dystopian futurist romances, of both serious literature and the most formulaic of popular romance. There was no name for it until Hugo Gernsback dubbed it science fiction.

The Gothic Tradition: Science Fiction

The idea that science fiction is our century's version of Gothic literature has been advanced by a number of writers, often with the observation that Mary Shelley, in *Frankenstein,* wrote the first true science fiction novel. Certainly there are plenty of similarities between the two types on all levels to support this contention even without the linking example of *Frankenstein.* Writer and critic Brian Aldiss finds science fiction closely related to Gothic literature in its exotic settings, suspenseful action, and concern with the inexplicable. Two other strong links are the similarity of popular and critical reception accorded to both types, and the similar effects of public reaction upon both. Science fiction, like Gothic fiction, has enjoyed its greatest popularity with a relatively nonliterary audience, and was for a long time ignored by academic and critical establishments. The popularity of the form, by providing a fairly open and dependable market for short fiction during the middle of this century, ensured the publication of a great deal of work, much of it of uneven quality at best, but some of it artistically excellent. At the same time, the absence of criticism from outside the field tended for a long time to protect writers both from the improving objectivity that such criticism might provide and from the sometimes stultifying self-consciousness that flaws much serious mainstream writing.

The most striking resemblance between Gothic literature and science fiction, however, is the remarkable diversity of work that has been included under both labels. As with the Gothic, one can find various opinions about what constitutes science fiction. Strict constructionists would have it include *only* fiction that depends for one or more of its major elements upon a principle or theory of one of the biological or physical sciences. Thus, a love story involving two computer operators would qualify as science fiction only if the story somehow turned upon the operations of a computer; furthermore, the story would be *not* science fiction but fantasy if the computer did something patently impossible, such as revising the past (as in Stephen King's short story "Word Processor"). Such a strict interpretation of the term obviously poses difficulties, as what is regarded as possible—from Martian canals to faster-than-light travel—changes.

Such definitions are somewhat beside the point, in any case, as the science fiction label has been and probably will continue to be applied to fiction involving possible and (so far as anyone knows) impossible science and technology, time travel and "alternate" universes, also ghosts, vampires, werewolves, demons, dragons, statisticians—in short, Aldiss's inexplicable and more. As with any truly serious literature, formulaic or not and even in its most formulaic phases, while science fiction may have included works that are less than serious and less than *true,* at its best it has always dealt, as Thomas D'Evelyn et al. say, with "things that may be unrealistic but are more real than a slice of life out of the Midwest" (24). And, like Gothic literature, science fiction is usually much easier to recognize than to define. This may be because both are really defined not by form but by function. Like Gothic literature, science fiction is literature that attempts, by the use of metaphoric structure and movement, to repair the fault in human consciousness, to reveal the relationship between what we are and what we think we are and wish to be. It is *monstrous* literature; it warns.

What science fiction writers have to say, as critics, about *Frankenstein* itself is revealing of what many of them seem to be about in their own work. This perspective on *Frankenstein* is well expressed in *Billion Year Spree* by Brian Aldiss, who maintains that Mary Shelley, influenced by the scientific interests of her contemporaries and her reading of Erasmus Darwin, brought the Gothic novel into the modern age by having Victor Frankenstein seek his fulfillment not through the medieval alchemists whose writings formed his boyhood reading—and, like Gothic forms in general, yearned toward the past—but through modern science. The creation of the Monster is a "perversion of the natural order" but is inevitable, given the evolution of human desire for knowledge, and is necessarily followed by "man's confrontation with himself" (Victor's confrontation with the Monster, his double) and by social upheaval and destruction (the Monster's destruction of

Victor's family) (27). In Aldiss's reading, the Monster represents scientific creation, humanity's technological progress leading through the Industrial Revolution into the twentieth century (for Aldiss believes that Mary Shelley's was a futuristic vision); and the corruption of technology—the Monster's turning to evil as his good—is a result of the inability of humanity to deal morally and ethically with its technological success.

Aldiss's assessment of Frankenstein is revealed more fully in his 1973 novel *Frankenstein Unbound,* at once a satire and a truly Gothic work of science fiction. It is cast in epistolary form, in the letters of one Joe Bodenland, a middle-aged Texan who finds himself "timeslipped" (an effect of superweaponry) from the year 2020 into a nineteenth century where Mary Shelley, Victor Frankenstein, and the Monster exist in equal reality— although Bodenland begins to suspect that reality in any case may mean that he is himself only a character in Aldiss's novel. The equal reality of creator and creature is for Aldiss at the thematic center of *Frankenstein,* and the instability of the world—the "perversion of the natural order"—apparently set in motion by the inventors of technology was in fact always inevitable, voluntarily determined, paradoxically a part of human nature. "From now onward," asks Victor Frankenstein, rhetorically, of Bodenland, "are all generations to feel guilty?...So much we have achieved, so much more is there to achieve. Must that achievement always carry the maggot of guilt in it? Or perhaps guilt has always been a condition of man..." (64). In his own Adam, in an essentially Godless world, Aldiss's version of Victor Frankenstein has discovered original sin.

The *science* of this first science fiction novel, Aldiss argues in his own novel, is not only that of Frankenstein's mysterious engine by which the Monster was set in motion in Mary Shelley's creative dream, but is above all the science of evolution, which was revealed to human beings even as their belief in God the Creator died. And the Monster was the precursor not only of generations of machines but also of those human beings who would soon live in a world controlled by the machine. In Aldiss's novel, the female monster is completed, and her face is the face of the dead Justine Moritz.

The frozen wasteland into which Bodenland pursues the pair of Monsters (having killed Victor and assumed his guilt) seems at first to be a part of the pre-human past, entered unwittingly through another timeslip. But as Bodenland approaches an immense walled city, he senses that he is actually in the far future and draws back. This is no human city, he feels, for the Monsters are making for it as if it were their home. "The future might be theirs and not ours," he thinks (219). In the end, Bodenland himself is the real monster, the only human being left (and his own humanity is in doubt) in a world alien to him, taking refuge in darkness and distance. Like Robert Neville in *The Omega Man* (a film version of Richard Matheson's *I Am Legend*), in which one man survives an epidemic blood disease that has turned the rest of humanity into vampires, Bodenland becomes the Gothic mirror image of himself.

Critical views of *Frankenstein* from other writers within the science fiction field tend in many cases to resemble Aldiss's, but often lack his criticism's complexity, interpreting the novel's central characters and events in a more nearly allegorical fashion. Victor, in these views, is the prototypical mad scientist, a stock science fiction figure who is unable to exert moral control over his efforts, himself controlled by paranoid delusions or, in some incarnations, by the political ambition or greed of others, the scientist himself being innocent of such worldly matters. The Monster is the prototypical robot, all power and no soul, turning on its creator because of something left out of—or underestimated in—its "character." Thus *Frankenstein* is for such writers essentially a cautionary tale, as are the science fiction productions that follow it and echo its theme. Again, the complexity of *Frankenstein* is better reflected in its influence upon fictional work, such as Richard Matheson's "Born of Man and Woman," in which the protagonist is a monstrous human child (never actually described, as the story is told from the child's point of view), chained by its parents in a damp cellar where pain teaches it to desire revenge; or Alfred Bester's "Fondly Fahrenheit," in which a robot's murderous madness is caused by faulty materials, a wire lacking resistance to heat, but is reflected in—or perhaps from—the madness of its owner who protects it from discovery and eventually assumes its "personality," including its inclination to mayhem in hot weather.

For those who see *Frankenstein* as primarily a science fiction novel, Mary Shelley's vision was of the future, and her precognition was the product of her education in Godwinian socialism and her intuition of scientific progress. The Monster is more than a psychological or philosophical construct, though his psychological and philosophical significance is unavoidable; the equal reality of creator and creature is central. The Monster's actions are separate from Frankenstein's, beyond his control though in a sense determined by him by virtue of his having designed the Monster, and they have real consequences in a real world. Technology is the doppelgänger, reflecting humanity's scientific achievement but also its moral inadequacies and its guilt.

The relationship between humanity and its scientific or technological creations—including its own changing nature—is a central concern, arguably *the* central concern, of science fiction. Several familiar Gothic characteristics are echoed within that theme, including exotic settings, reversals of expectations, the masculine/feminine dichotomy, and the doppelgänger.

The apparent removal of setting and situation from the world of the ordinary, limited in the traditional Gothic novel or romance to a few centuries' removal into the past and/or a romanticized exotic (e.g., Italian or North African) setting, is wholly unlimited in scope in science fiction; yet as in the Gothic this removal is only apparent. Characters and situations may exist a millenium or two in the fictional future, on an imaginary world or even in an imaginary universe, but science fiction—particularly "hard" science fiction— strives for verisimilitude and portrays characters who are very little different from their mainstream counterparts in romantic or realistic fiction; the situations they find themselves in may be mind-bendingly exotic, but the problems and solutions are distinctly human and generally reassuringly familiar.

Thus, for example, in Frank Herbert's *Dune* much of the realistic detail for which the book is praised, from the description of the spice as tasting like cinnamon to the Judeo-Christian-Islamic suggestions in the traditions of the planet's nomads, draws its strength from its half-familiarity to the reader. In fact, *Dune*—like a great deal of science fiction—is in part a deliberate near-allegory mirroring social concerns of its time and in part a work of prescience, reflecting concerns of a decade and more *after* it was published; yet it remains in part, too, a work that operates on an unconscious level, like the best Gothic literature achieving its power through the balance and fusion of familiar and exotic or weird elements and the introduction of traditional Gothic motifs or symbols, such as the labyrinthine underground dwellings of the Fremen, the suggestions and indirect presentations of incest, the human and nonhuman monsters, and the frankly Byronic hero.

The denial of accepted rational and moral "truths," often represented in the Gothic by the emergence of the villain or monster as a powerful force despite sentimental assurances that reason and good will prevail, is often ambiguously achieved in science fiction as in the Gothic. Especially before the 1960s, science itself was portrayed as the most rational of pursuits and was generally seen as heroic, the solution to all possible problems. Yet the mad scientist, a metaphor for rationality gone berserk, has remained from the Faustian tradition onward a central figure. Furthermore, again more frequently before the 1960s, science fiction traditionally reasserts conventional rational and moral principles just as the Gothic, in most instances, reasserts the sentimental world view—*after* the threatening element, the denial of convention, has been established as the work's most powerful and memorable figure.

For example, in *The Thing* (the 1951 film, adapted from John W. Campbell's short novel *Who Goes There?*), the scientist and the monster are actually in league, since the creature poses a danger only after it has— accidentally—been thawed from its ice block and, in addition to killing several people, has begun to reproduce, none of which would have taken place had the scientist not insisted upon studying the monster. With the help of the scientist's female assistant, the army officer who is the film's protagonist manages to destroy the monster only after the monster has killed the scientist. The creature, portrayed as an irrational, amoral, inexorable power bent on propagating itself (the political analogy in this Cold War-era film was clear), cannot be effectively dealt with by the use of reason or conventional morality, and the scientist's efforts are seen as naïve and finally sinister; only the enlightened, "sane" technology employed by the military is effective. But even after the creature is destroyed, the film ends (as do many Gothic novels) ambiguously, with the warning that other such creatures may appear, that humanity must "watch the skies!"

The masculine/feminine dichotomy, presented as a cultural imperative by the sentimental tradition and revealed in the Gothic as a metaphor for violent psychic dividedness, is also pervasive in science fiction. The monstrous or villainous force acting as a specific threat to feminine characters is, of course, a commonplace of "conventional" science fiction, as the half-serious, half-parodic tribute to this convention in the George Lucas film *Star Wars* reminds us. In fact, science fiction of the first half of this century is very little different from the typical Gothic novel in its portrayal of the heroine as potential victim; more recently, science fiction has largely abandoned the passive sentimental heroine, but the masculine/feminine dichotomy is still presented in a variety of subtle ways.

Again, *The Thing* provides useful examples of both the conventional monster/heroine conflict and other, less direct reminders of this dichotomy. The monster, presumably an alien from some culture technologically developed enough to have begun space travel, is seen throughout the film as a huge man-shaped creature without discernible features or apparent intellectual capacity, vaguely reminiscent, in form and movement, of the Boris Karloff portrayal of Frankenstein's Monster. Like the typical Gothic monster, the Thing so depletes of their masculine courage the men who are set to guard it that they cover its block of ice with a heated blanket and inadvertently bring it to life. The ensuing action includes the almost obligatory scene of the hero rescuing the heroine from the monster's path. However, this heroine is not so helpless and passive as the fainting ladies of Gothic literature, nor is the monster so obviously a conglomerate of excessively masculine traits that he prefers a feminine victim. In fact, *he* is apparently *it,* a vegetable that reproduces asexually, its offspring growing in pods in the greenhouse. Like Dracula, the Thing is a vampire, draining blood from its victims to fertilize its growing family, to which it is, like Victor Frankenstein to the Monster, both father and mother. The Thing is most frightening, then, in its reproductive capacity, its need for human warmth and blood to promulgate its own alien life. Ironically, the warmth and blood it requires to reproduce are in sharp contrast to the chilly, artificial courtship conducted between the hero and heroine in the Arctic cold of the military base.

The monster as both creature and creator illustrates the complexity with which both the masculine/feminine dichotomy and the doppelgänger motif are treated in modern science fiction. In Anthony Burgess's *A Clockwork Orange,* technological society—itself monstrous—has created the monster, Alex, whose equation of sexual pleasure and violence makes him both a vital and a sterile creature at once, a kind of vampire who is his own victim. Alex's blending of masculine and feminine traits is not a sign of the psychic unity the sentimental/Gothic myth both seeks and avoids; Alex is actually a kind of a fusion of Jekyll and Hyde, whose very essence is self-division. (The makeup Alex wears in the Stanley Kubrick film of Burgess's novel, with long, artificial lashes on *one* eye, suggests his dividedness.) Society then, divided against itself, re-creates Alex, reprograms him as one would a computer or a robot to become ill at the thought of sex or violence, and the novel's conflict becomes Alex's struggle, eventually successful, to overpower this conditioning. The Alex who emerges *is* unified, but he is not human—at least not as humanity is conventionally understood.

Like Aldiss, whose Monsters at the end of *Frankenstein Unbound* have apparently inherited the earth, Burgess suggests that science and human volition have combined to create the perfect monster, the perfect sex-and-violence machine. And, again like Aldiss, who implicates not only Frankenstein, the scientist, but Mary Shelley and himself, the artists, in the creation of the Monster, Burgess introduces his own doppelgänger, the novelist who is both Alex's victim and his creator, having survived Alex's crippling attack on him and his wife in their home (identified by a sign as "HOME") to become instrumental in his final "reprogramming." Both Burgess and Aldiss seem to be saying, among other things, that technological progress propagates, rather than overcomes, our society's self-divisions, that technology and art are *both* reflections of a culture's character, and that society uses its creations in acts of sexual violence and sexual revenge that are finally self-destructive.

While its settings may be in the near or far future or in the mythic or alternate past, science fiction differs from much of the Gothic in its being a futurist literature, a warning of what may be as much as of what is—although, as its best practitioners from Mary Shelley to Anthony Burgess demonstrate, the age of science *is* the age of the future because every act carries itself on giant steps into its consequences. Thus it is not surprising that, as critics Robert Scholes and Eric S. Rabkin put it, science fiction itself took a long stride in about the middle of the twentieth century into "a new literary self-consciousness and a new social awareness" (88). Science fiction has become much more sophisticated and consciously introspective in the past quarter-century, much more aware of and in step with mainstream literary movements, more respectable. These changes have affected the way Gothic themes and symbols are presented. One of the most basic and important changes in recent science fiction is that pervasive sentimental/Gothic metaphors like the masculine/feminine dichotomy and the doppelgänger have become more often frankly symbolic, deliberate figures for the divided self and for the existential encounter with the Other. Two of Ursula K. LeGuin's stories, originally published in 1969 and 1971, illustrate this development.

"Nine Lives," a story LeGuin describes as "a working out of a theme directly extrapolated from contemporary work in one of the quantitative sciences," explores concepts of self and nonself, love, and the substitution of self-division for encounters with other people. The doppelgänger in this story is literal: a ten-person clone trained as mining engineers, sent to work on an inhospitable planet whose only inhabitants are a geologist and a cartographer. The members of the clone—all named John Chow, with individual middle names that are actually letters of the Hebrew alphabet—are "doubles by duplication," grown from tissue taken from a young mathematician after his accidental death. (The rationale for cloning is the loss of most of Earth's population in famines.) Alvaro Martin and Owen Pugh, the two men who have charted the planet and discovered the mine, and in the meantime established a close if tense and somewhat unequal relationship between themselves, are at once jealous of and put off by the oneness of the John Chows; not only is the clone so self-sufficient and self-involved that they pay little attention to Martin and Pugh, but they are entirely open about their sexual self-involvement (the clone is half male, half female), prompting Pugh to wonder if they are committing incest or masturbation, and causing the two "single" men to become edgy and short-tempered. Thus, the conflict as the story begins seems to be between Pugh and Martin as well as between the two of them and the clone. The major plot complication occurs, however, when nine members of the clone are killed in an earthquake that collapses the mineshaft. The surviving member, Kaph, seems permanently traumatized; the story then focuses on his struggle to survive and emerge as an individual being in a world of other people.

One is reminded of Sartre's statement, in *No Exit,* that "hell is other people"; LeGuin's planet is a hellish place, with constant quakes, volcanic eruptions, and an unbreathable atmosphere, and Martin has named the mine Hellmouth. In a dream, on the first night after the clone's arrival, Pugh is chased by a "one-eyed giant" through a labyrinthine hell. Polyphemus, the ancient mythic monster who ate Odysseus's crew, may be a premonition of the nine John Chows' fate, but is in any case a figure for the stranger, the Other who threatens the identity and thus the existence of the self. Although the monster of "Nine Lives" at first appears to be the clone, the literally "self-devoted" plural stranger who needs nothing from others and gives nothing to them, it becomes clear as the story develops that the planet (a figure for the human condition) is the real monster. The planet (and by extension the mining company and the social structure that counts mineral wealth as more valuable than human life—the capitalist world) forces those who work on it to isolate themselves from the rest of society not only by distance but also by time, for they are light-years from Earth. And the planet further isolates and threatens to isolate them from each other, killing Kaph's nine siblings, and nearly killing Martin in the climactic episode that finally rouses Kaph from his zombielike state as he recognizes the possibility of love, the nature of a human relationship that cannot exist between the members of one self-divided individual. Ironically, the planet is named Libra, its constant turbulence suggesting the turbulent, give-and-take relationships between human beings by which a balance is finally achieved.

The balance struck between Pugh and Martin is a delicate and uneven one. Pugh (the more conventionally feminine of the two, though the relationship is *not* homoerotic) gives more than he takes, and is unresentfully aware of it, but the balance is lasting and satisfying for both. LeGuin suggests that a perfect relationship, the unity of the clone, is possible—indeed, that it can exist whenever human beings substitute self-sufficiency for love and deal with each other on a superficial level. But such a relationship is solipsistic, sterile. This is shown both symbolically, in that the women of the clone are genetically unable to reproduce, and literally, in that the clone's members think and react alike. Martin and Pugh suspect that this is why none of the John Chows who were in the mine at the beginning of the quake managed to escape. The relationship between Pugh and Martin is imperfect, and will always be so, because individuals are always solitary, always essentially strangers. At most, LeGuin says, they can see each other occasionally, occasionally touch. Thus, paradoxically, perhaps hell *is* other people—but the effort, always frightening and always futile, to reveal oneself completely to the other, to give up one's identity, is the only way and the only reason for human beings to live.

In a later story, "Vaster than Empires and More Slow," LeGuin again explores the paradoxical urge toward and straining away from unity with the Other—the problem that Masao Miyoshi has called the "Romantic paradox." Here she presents a monster in a society of monsters, an "empath" who has joined a crew of planetary explorers sent light-centuries from their own time to report on possible inhabited worlds. This person, a man named Osden, has been cured of a previously incurable form of autism by a famous psychiatrist who theorized that his condition was caused by a "supernormal empathic capacity"—a power to read the emotions of others—which forced Osden as an infant to turn totally inward in self-defense. Now Osden has been accepted as a member of an exploration crew entirely composed of neurotics (normal people refuse to travel so far into the future). By the time they arrive at their destination, a planet that apparently has no intelligent life—indeed no animal life—at all, Osden's "creator," the only person with whom he can live without suffering, is long dead, and Osden has reflected the others' abnormal emotional reactions so faithfully that they all despise him—which, of course, he feels and echoes back to them.

The rest of the crew, as individuals, have worked out more or less supportable relationships among themselves, but they are nearly at the point of murdering Osden when they find they are all subject to a sudden, almost unbearable anxiety apparently emanating from the planet itself. It turns out that the planet's plant life is a network making up one great emotional entity, completely alien to the human beings (a "vegetable emotion"—thus the allusion to Marvell's poem in the story's title). This entity, having evolved in absolute solitude, is as empathic as Osden and is reacting to the presence of other individuals with such terrible fear that it threatens to overpower not only Osden but, through him, the entire crew. The solution, arrived at by Osden in temporary sympathy with the crew chief Tomiko (who has been able to reverse her hatred of him through an understanding of his suffering) is that Osden will recapitulate on a large scale what he and Tomiko have managed only temporarily and slightly to accomplish—he will allow empathy, the understanding of the Other, to invade his own identity; Osden will become the Other, and it will become Osden. Tomiko pilots a plane carrying Osden to the center of the "forest," Osden alights and disappears, and in a moment the fear that has been communicating itself to the crew in terrible waves is gone.

Osden's solution is, in fact, the solution proposed by Frankenstein's Monster to the problems that plagued him and his creator: "Make me happy and I shall again be virtuous." But the difference between Osden's situation and Frankenstein's is significant. The proposal is actually made—suggested emotionally—by the planet, but it can only be conceptualized and carried out by Osden, who is able to recognize, in the planet's fear of him, the reflection of his own fear. The planet, neither masculine nor feminine (the absence of animal life makes sexual reproduction through fertilization impossible; there are no flowers), is purely emotional and at the mercy of the human explorers; it is as if the Monster had been imprinted with Victor's first terrified reaction and had carried that fear and horror away with him (which, in a sense, he has—his ugliness, which causes the DeLaceys and others to fear him, is the result of Victor's emotional abhorrence of him during the act of his creation).

But Osden himself is a monster, created by the psychiatrist who cured him of autism and forced him to experience the world of human relationships without the escape of solitude. Osden's creation of the planet-monster—and by extension *every* encounter between human strangers—is precisely a recapitulation or model of the psychiatrist's creation of Osden. Unlike Victor Frankenstein, Osden is able to recognize his own monstrousness and can thus empathize with the planet, the monster that he has created by discovering it emotionally and inadvertently allowing it to discover him.

Victor Frankenstein's heroism lies in his tragically successful effort to maintain his prescribed conscious identity, his sentimental masculinity which is the only *self* his culture allows him—an effort that deprives him of self-unity and thus of the possibility of love, of unity with others. Osden's heroism, in LeGuin's story, is exactly the opposite. In giving up his conscious identity to the Other, he paradoxically achieves unity—with the planet, but also with the crew and with himself, for the cessation of fear that the crew feels signals that both the planet and Osden have been released from the terrible anxiety of isolation and confrontation with the stranger. Osden has been able to accomplish this release of self and simultaneous achievement of self because he could consciously recognize himself in the mirror of the Other, as Victor could not. Again, as in "Nine Lives," LeGuin implies that such a relationship is achieved through oscillation, a balance *(libra)* between two personalities: "a slow resonance of feeling, a consonance of trust, a harmony" (210). This resonance, this balance, could never have taken place between two polarized, static individuals each committed to a role, an artificial concept of self.

Martin and Pugh, in "Nine Lives," are closely involved with each other in a nonsexual relationship, but the masculine and feminine elements within both—Martin's machismo and his insecurity, Pugh's emotional strength and physical weakness—allow them to resonate, to balance each other emotionally. The relationship between Osden and the empathic planet cannot be in any way sexual, yet it is a relationship in which activity and passivity, strength and weakness, masculinity and femininity as these terms have come to be defined, must resonate between both individuals. LeGuin's point, made in these two short stories as well as in her novels *The Left Hand of Darkness* and *The Dispossessed,* is that traits we think of as masculine and feminine are all human traits, all possessed to some degree by every person regardless of sex, that these traits must interact and balance for human beings to love each other, and that to love each other is the only way for human beings to survive.

Having come this far in tracing sentimental and Gothic themes in romance and science fiction, the twentieth-century successors of and equivalents to sentimental/Gothic literature, we must recognize that the difference in treatment of these themes is more than superficial, more than the mere shift in perspective from past to future, in the science fiction of the second half of this century. Novels like *Frankenstein Unbound* and *A Clockwork Orange* and films like *The Omega Man* are still warnings of the possible consequences for humanity if the sentimental/Gothic split in consciousness is preserved in its technological reflections, but such works seem to suggest that this outcome in inevitable, that whatever unity eventually results will be an apocalyptic unity beyond human experience or comprehension. Whether this is expressed in terms of a world of vampires, of an irrational destruction of the space-time continuum and a city of monsters, of Alex's casting off of his conditioning, or of the literal destruction of the human race on earth, it amounts to the same thing: the end of human civilization. On the other hand, writers like LeGuin who postulate a possible *healing* of human dividedness see this outcome as achievable only on an individual level, or as taking place among human survivors of an apocalyptic catastrophe, or as possible in understanding but not in practice.

In either view, the futuristic vision of science fiction has become less a warning of what may be than a foretelling of what *will* be. Joe Bodenland in 2020 can foresee the future but cannot change it. Alex, who retains his human will despite his having been made a machine, can use it only to become a self-directed machine. Neville, in *The Omega Man,* realizes that he himself, the last human survivor, is the stranger, the monster. Martin and Pugh, together with Kaph, who may go with them to survey another planet, have achieved the delicate balance of love but are still essentially strangers; Pugh, exhausted after rescuing Martin, is asleep and does not hear Kaph's "Good night," a "benediction" pronounced in the dark. Tomiko realizes that there will not be time—that perhaps in human lifetimes there cannot be time—for the resonance of love to occur between herself and Osden.

As science fiction in the twentieth century moves into a literary and social awareness of itself as part of the technological and artistic mirror of our culture, both facets of this evolution act together in an apparent bringing of the sentimental/Gothic division into consciousness, a development which to some extent must necessarily function as a healing of this essentially conscious/unconscious division. At the same time, traditional science fiction seems to be moving into mainstream literature or into a subcategory of its own, while a popular audience grows for heroic fantasy, a self-consciously mythic representation of sentimental, Gothic, and realistic themes in deliberately nonrealistic, romantic terms. On the other hand, another possible subcategory of science fiction, close to the traditionally Gothic novel in its realistic presentation and tale of terror atmosphere, is the contemporary horror novel or film.

From the early 1970s to the middle 1980s in cinema and popular novels, this subgenre has continued to demonstrate our culture's self-division, its insistence despite considerable relaxation upon sexual roles and identities, with a basically unconscious but artistically sure use of symbolism that affects readers as strongly and as surely as the Gothic always has done. The crew of a merchant spaceship, unknowingly "programmed" by the company that employs them to bring back any alien life form they discover regardless of the cost in human lives, is destroyed systematically, in the 1979 film *Alien,* by a distinctly nonhumanoid but certainly phallically suggestive monster. The Alien has gained entrance to their ship by impregnating, through the mouth, one of the crew members; having fed on this man's living body during an apparent larval stage, it bursts upward through his torso in a grisly scene and proceeds to stalk the crew through the ship's corridors, growing quickly to gigantic size and devouring the protagonists one by one until it is finally destroyed by the last surviving crew member, Ripley, who compulsively sings "You are ... My lucky star" as she flushes the creature into space. In the same film, the science officer, who appears to be the mad scientist or Frankenstein figure until his monstrous android nature is revealed, has permitted the monster to live, attached to its unfortunate host; the android is the only crew member who knows the secret order that mandates the creature's survival. Injured slightly during a scuffle with Ripley, he becomes truly mad—the machine gone berserk, in the manner of *2001's* computer HAL—and attempts to kill Ripley by stuffing a rolled-up porno magazine (believe it or not) down her throat, before he literally comes apart, leaking milklike fluid from his "wounds."

In Stephen King's *Cujo* (1981), two married couples, locked into patterns of domesticity in which human love and hypocrisy are helplessly confused, act out a chain of events that creates a monster—a rabid pet dog—and ends in the death of one couple's child. (The dog, in a "foreword" to the novel, is bitten by a bat in an underground cavern, but the actions and inaction of the human protagonists are what permit its madness to develop into a murderous force.) As usual in his fiction, King implies that evil is a kind of field that gathers and takes physical shape in the presence of human greed, hypocrisy, lust, and loneliness. In *Cujo* there is no supernatural, paranormal, or science fiction element, yet the Gothic power of the monster—which is at the same time a dumb, suffering, domestic pet—is undeniable.

Yet even these more widely popular recent manifestations of the Gothic tradition suggest, in their characterizations and plots, that a healing of the sentimental/Gothic division is at least theoretically possible. In *Cujo,* the parents whose child has died recognize their own culpability, and the novel ends with their recommitment to each other. In *Aliens,* the 1986 sequel in which Ripley destroys the *mater generis* of the alien species by blowing an entire planet out of the sky with nuclear weaponry, she and Newt, the little girl whom she has rescued (*newt:* salamander, a mythically self-perpetuating creature generated in fire), are saved by an android who destroys himself physically for their sakes and proves himself truly human—or perhaps gains his humanity—in doing so.

Thus, popular Gothic fiction—recent horror films and novels as well as recent science fiction—appears to be signaling an end, at least a possible end, to the sentimental/Gothic breach in consciousness that has dominated Western culture for so long. Modern writers more than ever seem to be following the lead of Mary Shelley in drawing our awareness, conscious and unconscious, to the tragic nature and consequences of this division, in attempting, as W. H. Auden says of Freud, to

> ... unite
> The unequal moieties fractured
> By our own well-meaning sense of justice,
> [To] restore to the larger the wit and will
> The smaller possesses but can only use
> For arid disputes, [to] give back to
> The son the mother's richness of feeling.
> But [to] have us remember most of all
> To be enthusiastic over the night...
> [whose creatures] too would rejoice
> If allowed to serve enlightenment....
> ("In Memory of Sigmund Freud," lines 90–106)

Whether or not twentieth-century humanity on earth can benefit in any practical way from its warnings, surely by a clearer understanding of the literature of the sentimental/Gothic myth we can, as individuals, allow the creatures of our own nightmares, the monsters in our own mirrors, "to serve enlightenment."

Works Cited

Books and Articles

Alcott, Louisa May. *Little Women.* New York: Grossett and Dunlap, 1915.

Aldiss, Brian W. *Billion Year Spree: The True History of Science Fiction.* Garden City: Doubleday, 1973.

_____. *Frankenstein Unbound.* Greenwich, Conn.: Fawcett, 1975. (Originally published by Random House, 1973.)

Auden, W. H. "The Christian Tragic Hero: Contrasting Captain Ahab's Doom and Its Classic Greek Prototype." *The New York Times Book Review* 7 (December 16, 1945), 1, 26.

_____. "In Memory of Sigmund Freud." *The Collected Poetry of W. H. Auden.* New York: Random House, 1945.

Austen, Jane. *Northanger Abbey.* John Davie, ed. London, New York: Oxford University Press, 1971.

_____. *Pride and Prejudice.* Frank W. Bradbrook, ed. London, New York: Oxford University Press, 1970.

Bate, Walter Jackson. *From Classic to Romantic: Premises of Taste in Eighteenth Century England.* Cambridge, Mass.: Harvard University Press, 1949.

Bester, Alfred. "Fondly Fahrenheit." *The Magazine of Fantasy and Science Fiction* (October 1979), 12–28. (First published in *The Magazine of Fantasy and Science Fiction,* Summer 1950.)

Bettelheim, Bruno. *The Uses of Enchantment: The Meaning and Interpretation of Fairy Tales.* New York: Knopf, 1977.

Bloom, Harold. *The Ringers in the Tower: Studies in the Romantic Tradition.* Chicago and London: University of Chicago Press, 1971.

Brontë, Charlotte. *Jane Eyre.* New York: New American Library, Signet Classics, 1960.

Burgess, Anthony. *A Clockwork Orange.* New York: Norton, 1963.

Campbell, John W. "Who Goes There?" In *The Best of John W. Campbell,* Lester del Ray, ed. New York: Nelson Doubleday, 1976.

D'Evelyn, Thomas, et al. "From Apocalyptic Novels to 'Beige' Notes." *Christian Science Monitor* October 9, 1986, 21–24.

Dickens, Charles. *Bleak House.* Duane DeVries, ed. New York: Crowell, 1971.

_____. *Great Expectations.* New York: Dodd, Meade and Co., 1942.

Ellis, Kate. "Monsters in the Garden: Mary Shelley and the Bourgeois Family." In *The Endurance of Frankenstein,* George Levine and U. C. Knoepflmacher, eds. Berkeley, Los Angeles, London: University of California Press, 1979, pp. 123–42.

Fiedler, Leslie. *Love and Death in the American Novel.* New York: Criterion, 1960.

Fleck, P. D. "Mary Shelley's Notes to Shelley's Poems and *Frankenstein.*" *Studies in Romanticism* 6 (Summer 1967), 226–54.

Golden, Morris. *Richardson's Characters.* Ann Arbor, Mich.: University of Michigan Press, 1963.

Hawthorne, Nathaniel. *The House of the Seven Gables.* Fredson Bowers, ed. Columbus: Ohio State University Press, 1965.

———. *The Scarlet Letter.* Fredson Bowers, ed. Columbus: Ohio State University Press, 1962.

Herbert, Frank. *Dune.* New York: Chilton, 1965.

Herold, J. Christopher. *Mistress to an Age.* New York: Time-Life Books, Bobbs-Merrill, 1958.

Hill, Christopher. "Clarissa Harlow and Her Times." In *Samuel Richardson: A Collection of Critical Essays,* John Carroll, ed. Englewood Cliffs, N.J.: Prentice-Hall, 1969, pp. 102–23.

Jennings, Richard. *La Fenêtre Gothique: The Influence of Tragic Form on the Structure of the Gothic Novel.* Dissertation, Muncie, Ind.: Ball State University, 1982.

Jung, C. G. *Archetypes of the Collective Unconscious.* New York: Pantheon, 1959.

Kaplan, Morton and Robert Kloss. *The Unspoken Motive: A Guide to Psychoanalytic Literary Criticism.* New York: Free Press, 1973.

Ketterer, David. *Frankenstein's Creation: The Book, the Monster, and Human Reality.* Victoria, B.C.: University of Victoria, 1979.

King, Steven. *Cujo.* New York: Viking, 1981.

———. *The Stand.* Garden City, N.Y.: Doubleday, 1978.

Knoepflmacher, U. C. "Thoughts on the Aggression of Daughters." In *The Endurance of Frankenstein,* George Levine and U. C. Knoepflmacher, eds. Berkeley, Los Angeles, London: University of California Press, 1979, pp. 88–119.

LeGuin, Ursula K. "Nine Lives." In *The Wind's Twelve Quarters.* New York, Evanston, San Francisco, London: Harper & Row, 1975, pp. 129–60.

———. "Vaster than Empires and More Slow." In *The Wind's Twelve Quarters.* New York, Evanston, San Francisco, London: Harper & Row, 1975, pp. 181–217.

Levine, George. "The Ambiguous Heritage of Frankenstein." In *The Endurance of Frankenstein,* George Levine and U. C. Knoepflmacher, eds. Berkeley, Los Angeles, London: University of California Press, 1979, pp. 3–30.

Lewis, M. G. *The Monk.* New York: Grove, 1952.

Matheson, Richard. "Born of Man and Woman." *The Magazine of Fantasy and Science Fiction* (October 1979), 150–52. (First published in *The Magazine of Fantasy and Science Fiction,* Summer 1950.)

———. *I Am Legend.* Garden City: Doubleday, 1954.

Maturin, Charles Robert. *Melmoth the Wanderer.* Douglas Grant, ed. London, New York: Oxford University Press, 1968.

Millet, Kate. *Sexual Politics.* New York: Doubleday, 1969.

Mitchell, Margaret. *Gone With the Wind.* New York: Macmillan, 1964.

Miyoshi, Masao. *The Divided Self: A Perspective on the Literature of the Victorians.* New York: New York University Press; London: University of London Press, 1969.

Moers, Ellen. "Female Gothic." In *The Endurance of Frankenstein,* George Levine and U. C. Knoepflmacher, eds. Berkeley, Los Angeles, London: University of California Press, 1979, pp. 77–87.

Nelson, Lowry, Jr. "Night Thoughts on the Gothic Novel." *Yale Review* 52 (Winter 1963), 236–57.

Praz, Mario. *The Romantic Agony.* Second edition. Angus Davison, trans. London, New York, Toronto: Oxford University Press, 1951.

Railo, Eino. *The Haunted Castle.* London: George Routledge and Sons; New York: E. P. Dutton, 1927.

Richardson, Samuel. *Clarissa.* Abridged and edited by Philip Stevick. San Francisco: Rinehart, 1971.

Rieger, James. "Introduction" to *Frankenstein, or, the Modern Prometheus,* by Mary Shelley. James Rieger, ed. The Library of Literature. Indianapolis, New York: Bobbs-Merrill, 1974.

Rigney, Barbara Hill. *Madness and Sexual Politics in the Feminist Novel.* Madison: University of Wisconsin Press, 1978.

Rogers, Robert. *A Psychoanalytic Study of the Double in Literature.* Detroit: Wayne State University Press, 1970.

Rougemont, Denis de. *Love in the Western World.* Montgomery Belgion, trans. New York: Harcourt Brace, 1940.

Rowe, Karen E. "Feminism and Fairy Tales." In *Women's Studies* 6 (1979).

Saxon, Martha. *Louisa May: A Modern Biography of Louisa May Alcott.* Boston: Houghton Mifflin, 1977.

Schaefer, Jack. *Shane.* Boston: Houghton Mifflin, 1982 (1949).

Scholes, Robert and Eric S. Rabkin. *Science Fiction: History, Science, Vision.* New York: Oxford University Press, 1977.

Shelley, Mary Wollstonecraft. *Frankenstein, or, the Modern Prometheus.* M. K. Joseph, ed. London, Oxford, New York: Oxford University Press, 1971.

Shelley, Percy Bysshe. *Alastor; or, the Spirit of Solitude. The Complete Poetical Works of Percy Bysshe Shelley,* Thomas Hutchinson, ed. London: Oxford University Press, 1960.

Small, Christopher. *Ariel Like a Harpy: Shelley, Mary, and Frankenstein.* London: Victor Gollancz Ltd., 1972.

Spark, Muriel. *Child of Light: A Reassessment of Mary Wollstonecraft Shelley.* Hadleigh, Essex: Tower Bridge Publications, 1951.

Sterrenburg, Lee. "Mary Shelley's Monster: Politics and Psyche in *Frankenstein.*" In *The Endurance of Frankenstein,* George Levine and U. C. Knoepflmacher, eds. Berkeley, Los Angeles, London: University of California Press, 1979, pp. 143–71.

Stevick, Philip. *"Frankenstein and Comedy."* In *The Endurance of Frankenstein,* George Levine and U. C. Knoepflmacher, eds. Berkeley, Los Angeles, London: University of California Press, 1979, pp. 221–39.

Stoker, Bram. *Dracula.* New York and Scarborough, Ontario: New American Library, 1965.

Thackeray, William M. *Vanity Fair.* M. R. Ridley, ed. New York: Dutton, 1970.

Thornburg, Thomas R. *The Quester and the Castle: The Gothic Novel as Myth, with Special Reference to Bram Stoker's* Dracula. Dissertation. Muncie, Ind.: Ball State University, 1970.

Tymms, Ralph. *Doubles in Literary Psychology.* Cambridge, England: Bowes and Bowes, 1949.

Van Ghent, Dorothy. *The English Novel: Form and Function.* New York: Harper & Row, 1961.

Varma, Devendra P. *The Gothic Flame.* New York: Russell and Russell, 1964.

Veeder, William. *Mary Shelley and Frankenstein: The Fate of Androgyny.* Chicago and London: University of Chicago Press, 1986.

Waldron, R. A., ed. *Sir Gawain and the Green Knight.* Evanston: Northwestern University Press, 1970.

Wiggin, Kate Douglas. *Mother Carey's Chickens.* New York: Grosset and Dunlap, 1910.

Wilt, Judith. *"Frankenstein as Mystery Play."* In *The Endurance of Frankenstein,* George Levine and U. C. Knoepflmacher, eds. Berkeley, Los Angeles, London: University of California Press, 1979, pp. 31–48.

Films

Alien. Ridley Scott, director. Gordon Carroll, David Giley, and Walter Hill, producers, for Twentieth-Century-Fox, 1979.

Aliens. James Cameron, director. Gale Anne Hurd, producer, for Twentieth-Century-Fox, 1986.

A Clockwork Orange. Stanley Kubrick, producer and director, for Warner Bros., 1971.

Shane. George Stevens, producer and director, for Paramount Pictures, 1952

Star Wars. George Lucas, director. Gary Kurtz, producer, for Twentieth-Century-Fox, 1977.

The Thing. Christian Nyby, director. Howard Hawks, producer, for RKO/Radio, 1951.

Works Consulted

Amis, Kingsley. *New Maps of Hell: A Survey of Science Fiction*. New York: Harcourt Brace, 1960.

Bataille, Georges. *Death and Sensuality*. New York: Ballantine Books, 1969 (ca. 1962).

_____. *Literature and Evil*. Alastair Hamilton, trans. New York: Urizen Books, 1973 (1957).

Campbell, Joseph. *The Masks of God: Primitive Mythology*. New York: Viking, 1968.

Church, Richard. *Mary Shelley*. London: Gerald Howe, 1928.

DeCamp, L. Sprague. *Science Fiction Handbook*. New York: Hermitage House, 1953.

el-Shatar, Safaa. *The Novels of Mary Shelley*. Salzburg: Institut für Englische Sprache und Literatur, 1977.

Frazer, Sir James George. *The Golden Bough: A Study in Magic and Religion*. Third edition. New York: Macmillan, 1951.

Freud, Sigmund. *The Intepretation of Dreams*. James Strachey, trans. and ed. New York: Avon, 1965.

Glut, Donald F. *The Frankenstein Legend*. Metuchen, N.J.: Scarecrow, 1973.

Graves, Robert. *The White Goddess*. Amended and enlarged edition. New York: Farrar, Straus and Giroux, 1966.

Grylls, Rosalie Glynn. *Mary Shelley: A Biography*. London, New York: Oxford University Press, 1938.

Hill, J. M. "Frankenstein and the Physiognomy of Desire." *American Imago* 32 (1975), 332–58.

Holmes, Richard. *Shelley: The Pursuit*. London: Weidenfeld and Nicolson, 1974.

Kiely, Robert. *The Romantic Novel in England*. Cambridge, Mass.: Harvard University Press, 1972.

Knight, Damon. *In Search of Wonder: Essays on Modern Science Fiction*. Second (revised) edition. Chicago: Advent, 1967.

LaValley, Albert J. "The Stage and Film Children of Frankenstein: A Survey." In *The Endurance of Frankenstein*, George Levine and U. C. Knoepflmacher, eds. Berkeley, Los Angeles, London: University of California Press, 1979, pp. 243–89.

Lipartito, Janice Dawson. "The Forms of the Beloved Dead: Frankenstein's Compulsive Quest for Unity in Death." Thesis. Muncie, Ind.: Ball State University, 1982.

Lyles, W. H. *Mary Shelley: An Annotated Bibliography*. Garland Reference Library of the Humanities, vol. 22. New York and London: Garland, 1975.

Mays, Milton. *"Frankenstein:* Mary Shelley's Black Theodicy." *Southern Humanities Review* 3 (Spring 1969), 146–53.

Neumann, Bonnie Rayford. *The Lonely Muse: A Critical Biography of Mary Wollstonecraft Shelley*. Salzburg: Institut für Anglistik und Amerikanistik, 1979.

Nitchie, Elizabeth. *Mary Shelley: Author of Frankenstein*. New Brunswick, N.J.: Rutgers University Press, 1953.

Philmus, Robert M. *Into the Unknown: The Evolution of Science Fiction from Francis Godwin to H. G. Wells*. Berkeley, Los Angeles: University of California Press, 1970.

Reiman, Donald, ed. *The Romantics Reviewed*. New York, London: Garland, 1972.

Scott, Peter Dale. "Vital Artifice: Mary, Percy, and the Psychopolitical Integrity of *Frankenstein*." In *The Endurance of Frankenstein*, George Levine and U. C. Knoepflmacher, eds. Berkeley, Los Angeles, London: University of California Press, 1979, pp. 172–202.

Shelley, Mary Wollstonecraft. *Frankenstein, or, the Modern Prometheus*. James Rieger, ed. The Library of Literature. Indianapolis, New York: Bobbs-Merrill, 1974.

––––––. *The Letters of Mary W. Shelley*. Frederick L. Jones, ed. Norman: University of Oklahoma Press, 1944.

––––––. *Mary Shelley's Journal*. Frederick L. Jones, ed. Norman: University of Oklahoma, Press, 1947.

Smith, Susan Harris. "*Frankenstein:* Mary Shelley's Psychic Divisiveness." *Women and Literature* 5, No. 2 (Spring 1977), 42–53.

Spark, Muriel and Derek Stanford, eds. *My Best Mary: The Selected Letters of Mary Wollstonecraft Shelley*. London: Allan Wingate, 1953.

Summers, Montague. *A Gothic Bibliography*. New York: Russell and Russell, 1964 (1941).

Index